לכן זה היל"ו דוקים,

הגדרה לפנינו

יהודה

, ל' פרמי,
פילוד

7.4058 זה, לו,

A Star in the Darkness

A Star in the Darkness

Ruth Zeidman

First published **2000**

Copyright © 1998 by Ruth Zeidman
7 Yoel Street, Jerusalem, Israel
Tel: 02-5376163

Phototypeset at Targum Press

Published by:
Targum Press Inc.
22700 W. Eleven Mile Rd.
Southfield, Mich. 48034

Printed in Israel

ISRAEL MEIR LAU

Chief Rabbi of Israel

ישראל מאיר לאו

הרב הראשי לישראל

י״ב Elul, תשנ״ח
3 September, 1998
R-101-98

Mrs. Ruth Zeidman
Rechov Yoel 7
Jerusalem
ISRAEL

Dear Mrs. Zeidman:

I was personally touched upon reading your inspiring book "Light in the Darkness."

Included in the collection of youth literature available to the public today is a growing amount of stories depicting the history of the Holocaust. However, not for naught was your book chosen to be an integral part of the learning curriculum in the Israeli school system, and is currently being strongly considered for integration at American schools likewise.

The uniqueness of the book "Light in the Darkness" is that it documents the most emotional and heart rending chapter of your personal life, emphasizing the innumerable challenges you were faced with which you triumphed over by your perpetual faith in the Almighty. In addition, the book illuminates the glorious example of Jews who fought with all their might to maintain the image of man in the deepest valleys of death.

The many positive responses you have been receiving from readers, young and old testify to their deep identification with your powerful words and ascertain that the book is fulfilling its intent.

As one who personally experienced the horrors of the Holocaust at a tender age, I sincerely recommend to parents, educators and anyone dealing with the youth to adapt this book, thereby bonding today's generation with one of the most difficult chapters in the biography of the Jewish people.

Sincerely Yours,

Israel Meir Lau

Israel Meir Lau
Chief Rabbi of Israel

28 September 1998

To whom it may concern,

Mrs. Ruth Zeidman is a Holocaust survivor and a person who has dedicated many years, since her retirement from her professional work, to the memory of the Holocaust period and the education of the younger generation in Israel.

Her book, A Star in the Darkness, is a substantial contribution to the Holocaust literature and presents the misery and hardship of people who were inspired in dark times by strong beliefs in human values and the future.

I strongly recommend to publish the Star in the Darkness, which is popular reading in Hebrew, in the English language.

Sincerely,

Israel Gutman
Chief Historian of Yad Vashem

בס״ד

April 27, 1998

Ms. Ruth Zeidman
Rechov Joel 7
Jerusalem, Israel

Dear Ms. Zeidman,

Congratulations on your publication of **A Star in the Darkness.** It has been my privilege to read and study the manuscript and I was deeply moved by your courage and your faith against the back drop of depravity and inhumanity.

This is a very significant book for your people and educators. Your memoir provides echoes of a past filled with the beauty and strength of Jewish life in a world gone mad. In addition, your book provides young people in particular, with a Judaism worthy of identification, in spite of the horrors, and without compromising the integrity of history.

Working, as I do, on a daily basis, with students, teachers, and librarians from all venues of society, I am delighted to be able to recommend **A Star in the Darkness**, a light in the world of Holocaust literature for young people.

Sincerely,

Adaire Klein
Director of Library and Archival Services

AK:sm

To: Mrs. R. Zeidman
From: M. Avidan, Inspector of Chinuch Atzmai Schools

I wish to point out that you have here succeeded in describing, with a truly artistic hand, one of the darkest periods in world history and, on the other hand, the courage and faith of the believers and sons of believers whose souls remained great and whose qualities sterling even when the sword was at their throats.

Between the pages of the events described are strewn faith, thoughts, sayings, and ideas which penetrate to the depths of the soul, and it is these that give *A Star in the Darkness* an added dimension — a moral and educational message.

Please accept my esteem, congratulations, and best wishes,

M. Avidan
Inspector of Chinuch Atzmai

The Israel Ministry of Education has recommended that Ruth Zeidman's book, A Star in the Darkness, be included on the teaching syllabus in every school in the State of Israel.

IN MEMORY OF

MY HUSBAND
Natan Nechemia z"l

son of Yisrael Mordechai Zeidman,

who was suddenly taken from us on the Sabbath

day, 4 Av 5742/1982, in the synagogue, at the

time of the afternoon prayers.

Natan Nechemia was an exceptional man, a fine and noble spirit, beloved by all who knew him. He was outstandingly kind-hearted, a man of good deeds in the fullest sense, a good friend who rejoiced in the joy of his fellows and strove to ensure their well-being.

No one who turned to him for a favor or for advice was ever turned away. He was always willing to do his best — and that "best" was a great deal. He was a man of sharp intellect and wide knowledge in many spheres. His *responsa* and advice astounded everyone by their clarity and grasp of the essentials.

He was an outstanding son, and for over nineteen years he supported his mother and honored her in a manner which truly fulfilled the commandment to honor one's parents. He was also a model husband. Together we built our new home as a continuation of our original homes in Czenstochow, which had been destroyed by the Holocaust.

Natan Nechemia was a devoted father and a beloved grandfather, who gave of himself with a full heart and infinite patience. He was a man who radiated happiness to all his surroundings.

He set aside a portion of each day for the study of Torah. Every day, early in the morning, he would host a regular Torah study group in our house. To this day, the pleasant melody that he would sing rings in my ears and is lodged still deep within my heart.

The source of his joy stemmed from his gratitude to God and the recognition that He is Master of the World. Natan Nechemia's last words, spoken two hours before he passed away, were: "The Lord God guides the world" — these words were repeated several times, with an emphasis on every word.

In our hearts, he remains alive and his memory will never fade from our minds.

May his soul be bound up in the bond of life.

Foreword

Books on the Holocaust are memorial candles which can never be extinguished.

This book is different. It is not a candle but a torch, shedding light upon its readers, young and old.

The uniqueness of this book lies in its mood. Although Ruth suffered much hardship and pain in her youth, this book does not convey despondence. On the contrary, it is the Chassidic spirit from her home, the unique Jewish upbringing she received, and Ruth's own optimistic soul which leave their stamp upon the book. By the author's own admission, she has in fact remained the same idealistic young girl that she was then.

The story is replete with basic Jewish values, which, when seen through her candid and personal viewpoint, awaken deep empathy and respect. Firm belief in God, strong family ties, self-sacrifice for another, sanctification of life for a higher purpose — all of these are changed in this book from abstract principles to simple reality.

As a teacher of history, I am well aware of the difficulty involved in fostering identification between today's students and the Jews of the Holocaust, in showing the values which we share. It seems to me that through direct educational methods alone, there is no way to surmount these difficulties, and only indirect educational influence (i.e., literature) can help allay them.

The personal dimension in this story is very strong, and unites the stories of a family, a class, a group of friends, a ghetto, and a nation. This, too, is an important factor in history classes where, in attempting to present a broader, larger perspective on events, we all too often lose the personal element, which forms a deeper identification and understanding.

These attributes, in addition to the general readability of the book, guarantee that it will attract young people everywhere and open new horizons for them. They will find a window into a Jewish world that was — which is described so simply, yet so beautifully — and a window into the human soul and the power hidden within it to believe in the beautiful and the good, and to find these even in a world enveloped by darkness.

The sky and the clouds, the birds and the flowers, the sun, a warm hand, the smile of a child; it was in such everyday pleasures that young Rutka found her "star in the darkness." And although this book is sensitive and touching, it does not contain that over-emotionality which distances today's youth from most Holocaust literature.

The Holocaust and its preservation in the world's memory is a subject very close to my heart. I have taken specialized courses in this field, both as a student of the contemporary Judaism society and as a teacher in the Horeb school, Jerusalem. In my humble opinion, this book is an important contribution to the bookshelves of the Holocaust.

Esther Farbstein, Ph.D.
Coordinator of the Holocaust Studies Dept.
Michlala for Girls, Jerusalem

Preface

I was born in the city of Czenstochow in Poland. My parents, Rabbi Itzhak Meir Dziubas and Sarah (née Rotblatt), were kind-hearted, wealthy people who enjoyed a good reputation among both Jews as well as gentiles. They were always ready to help those in need, whether with money or in any other practical way.

Our lives were led in considerable comfort. We had resident domestic help, and our vacations were spent in a village deep in the heart of the country.

My childhood passed happily and I felt secure in the deep love, boundless affection, and wholehearted devotion which my parents, sisters, and brothers bestowed upon me.

There is a Polish proverb which says: "Childhood sketches out the life of every man, and although it itself is transient and fleeting, its mark remains forever."

Yes, I have pleasant memories of my childhood, and I inherited from my home a high standard of values. Friday nights, Shabbat evenings, and the many Jewish festivals, each with their abundance of guests whom my father would bring home from the synagogue — all of this remains deep in my heart, unforgettable and unforgotten.

The atmosphere in our home was truly wonderful. A relationship of respect and affection reigned there which extended to all members of the family.

Despite the smoke and fires of war, and in spite of the terrible suffering we underwent, I feel that I retain within me still the values my parents instilled so deep in my being, and these will remain with me forever. These were the solid foundations on which I was able to build, in time, my own married life and my own home, in which I was able to educate my children and convey to them those same values.

Over forty years have passed since the end of World War II, and those shreds of memory, all the events I experienced from the very first day of the war until its end, remained tucked away in a corner of my mind.

Many friends and acquaintances, who had heard parts of my story, encouraged me to put these memories into writing. For years I kept putting off the idea, claiming that I had no time for such an undertaking, but it's possible that no less a factor in my reluctance was the fear of reliving those painful memories.

Perhaps I would have continued in that vein indefinitely if not for a snowy Jerusalem day a couple of years ago, when I fell and broke my leg. Upon hearing that I would need to be confined to bed for a number of weeks, I said to my husband, "It's a sign from Heaven. Now I *have* to start writing."

And then, as if they had just been waiting all these years for their cue, the floodgates of memory opened. Despite the many years that had passed since these terrible events, I had no difficulty in deciphering their secret code, hearing anew voices from the distant past, and recording them for posterity. Some of the memories were so hard and painful that reliving them brought tears to my eyes. Yet, one of my teachers would always tell me that I was adept at "seeing the glass half full," and I have taken great pains to spare my readers depressing thoughts and impressions. By nature I am optimistic and have been blessed with a heart full of hope and faith. I have never been one to see the black side of things.

Therefore, although this book tells of one of the darkest periods in European Jewish history, I relate the events as I lived them — the sorrow and the joy intertwined, the bittersweet today together with an unvanquishable faith in a bright tomorrow.

I would like to think that this book will touch the soul of the reader and penetrate his consciousness with an awareness of Divine Providence, and a love for the Jewish people, as well as for the Land of Israel, which so many generations prayed and struggled to reach. May it teach the reader to realize always that there are those whose suffering is greater than his own — for both joy and sadness know no limits and are subject to no absolute laws. It is therefore incumbent upon us all to believe in a better future, to strengthen our souls, and to place our trust in the Creator of all.

Contents

Chapter One
    The Eve of the War 1

Chapter Two
    Hardships of Daily Life. 6

Chapter Three
    A White Arm Band and a Blue Star of David 10

Chapter Four
    Typhus 16

Chapter Five
    The Establishment of the Great Ghetto 21

Chapter Six
    The Rebbe of Piltz, Author of *"Siftei Tzadik"* 25

Chapter Seven
    Our New Home in the Ghetto 30

Chapter Eight
    The Noose Tightens 36

Chapter Nine
    The *Aktion* 40

Chapter Ten

    In the Bunker 46

Chapter Eleven

    By the Skin of Our Teeth 52

Chapter Twelve

    Terror in the Dark. 57

Chapter Thirteen

    In the Bakery 64

Chapter Fourteen

    My Sisters 68

Chapter Fifteen

    My Departure from the Bunker. 72

Chapter Sixteen

    The End of the Bunker 76

Chapter Seventeen

    Waiting for Our Parents 80

Chapter Eighteen

    Rumors from Auschwitz 86

Chapter Nineteen

    Liquidation of the Kindergarten 90

Chapter Twenty

    The Great Selection. 95

Chapter Twenty-one

    The Doctors Entrapped 99

Chapter Twenty-two

    Jaundice. 105

Chapter Twenty-three

    Last Greetings from Marilka. 108

Chapter Twenty-four
The Revolt. 114

Chapter Twenty-five
A Pall of Smoke over the Ghetto. 119

Chapter Twenty-six
My Mother's Wedding Ring. 124

Chapter Twenty-seven
At the Rakov Factory 128

Chapter Twenty-eight
At the Hasag Factory 132

Chapter Twenty-nine
Pesach 135

Chapter Thirty
The Transport from Pietrkow 140

Chapter Thirty-one
A Gun at My Head. 144

Chapter Thirty-two
The Transports from Lodz and Skarzysko 148

Chapter Thirty-three
The Bombing of Czenstochow 153

Chapter Thirty-four
The Train 157

Chapter Thirty-five
Ravensbruck. 161

Chapter Thirty-six
Hela's Illness 165

Chapter Thirty-seven
"Stop Thief". 169

Chapter Thirty-eight
Parting from Hela 173

Chapter Thirty-nine
Journey into the Unknown 177

Chapter Forty
Burgau Camp 181

Chapter Forty-one
Turkheim Camp 185

Chapter Forty-two
The Escape 189

Chapter Forty-three
In the Forest 193

Chapter Forty-four
Liberation 197

Chapter Forty-five
The End of the War and the Search for Relatives . . 202

Epilogue 211

Appendix I 215

Appendix II 218

Letters of Recommendation 227

Chapter One

The Eve of the War

August, 1939. The air was already heavy with the scent of war. I was walking with my father on Second Avenue in Czenstochow, where we lived. My father paused to read one of the large notices which announced mass conscription. His face grew solemn, for he knew only too well the meaning of the word "war."

I, on the other hand, was quite excited, although my joy was marred somewhat by the fact that this war would not be exclusively mine, as my friends, too, would have a share in the experiences that lay ahead.

In the courtyards of the houses, people had begun digging trenches as protection against the expected German air raids. My sister Rivka had been chosen by the local residents to represent the "Home Guard," and she bore on her left sleeve the armband she had received from the Polish Air Force. This armband served as a permit enabling the bearer to go anywhere at all, at any time.

Then, on Friday, September 1, the radio announced the approach of enemy warplanes: "Attention! Attention! A plane is passing." In response to these warnings, the population had to go out to the trenches, in strict compliance with the orders of the Home Guard, who were in charge of civilian defense.

Friday night, the evening of Shabbat. A starched, white linen tablecloth covered the table, and the eight-branched silver candelabrum sat on its large silver tray, along with two more silver candlesticks. My mother would always light ten candles, one for each member of the family. As usual, the house sparkled with cleanliness and light in honor of Shabbat. And yet, this night was not like other Shabbat nights — the atmosphere was different.

We ate our Shabbat meal in haste, without much appetite, and immediately went out into the street. A terrible sight met our eyes: men, women, and children, loaded with parcels and household items, were walking in a long, seemingly endless procession. Some were on foot, others on vehicles or carts drawn by oxen or horses. Still others pushed baby carriages and handcarts onto which they had piled their belongings, and on top of these, their children.

"Where are you headed?" we asked, dismayed.

"Forward," came the answer, indicating their unknown destination with a thrust of the head. "The Germans are coming, they will kill us all...."

In our own building, No. 20 Second Avenue, lived about forty families, most of them with several children, but also a few elderly couples whose children had already left home. When the rumors began to spread, most of these families prepared to flee. Thirty of the neighboring families now started an exodus of their own. My father, however, refused to drag his tender children into the unknown.

The procession of refugees went on and on, and we stood by, watching silently. Only towards dawn did we return home. Nobody chased me off to bed, even my little brothers, three-year-old Yisroelik and seven-year-old Chanoch, stayed up that night. Suddenly, all routine and discipline seemed meaningless.

A strange silence reigned all the next day, Shabbat. It was the kind of tense quiet you get before a storm.

A minyan (quorum) gathered in our house for prayers, and several neighbors stayed for the Shabbat meal. Although there were children among the guests, we had no heart to play. We were too afraid of the unknown, of that dreadful "something" which hung over our heads like a pall of smoke.

That Saturday night, just after the end of Shabbat, Czenstochow was bombed for the first time. The sky was suddenly lit up with red balloons which fell with a loud noise on houses and other targets. Shaking with fear, we held each other's hands by way of comfort until at last we fell asleep, fully dressed.

When we awoke, we learned that the Germans had occupied Czenstochow, and their troops had already entered the town. This was on Sunday, the 3rd of September, 1939.

By the next day, notices were posted all over town instructing the citizens: "Do not switch on any light after 6:00 P.M." "It is forbidden to go outside or to look out of the window after 6:00 P.M." "Anyone disobeying these orders will be shot!"

That same day, Germans burst into our yard, yelling: "All men outside!" My father and my brother Mendel were taken with the other men of the town to some unknown destination. We followed them at first for an hour or more until they disappeared from sight. We walked back along deserted streets, empty of human life. Only soldiers on tanks were to be seen, pointing their weapons at us. When we returned home the house was dark, yet we turned on no light. While we were still sitting gloomily in the darkness, there came a burst of gunfire from all directions, into the courtyard and the apartments. Scared to death, we flung ourselves under the beds and tables, feeling that this grim night would never end.

The next day, the Germans released a part of the gentiles who had been arrested. The Jews were taken to the new marketplace and forced to stand the entire day with their hands above their heads, without food or water. Later, they were taken to a large church that stood in the center of the "New Market." Here they received orders to lie on the floor while the Germans amused themselves by taking random shots at them. Anyone who raised his head, even by a few centimeters, was hit. Screams sounded from the prostrate Jews, joining in one mighty cry, the cry of generations of Jews who have been persecuted and murdered for no crime other than their being Jewish: "Hear O Israel, the Lord our God...is One!"

There was no doubt in the hearts of the men that these were their last moments on earth and that the Germans, in their vile games, would finish them off. However, by the next day it became clear that while some men had indeed been killed or injured in that night of blood, the survivors would be permitted to return home.

As long as I live I shall never forget the sight of my father when he came back to us that morning. He was forty-six years old, but his black beard had turned grey overnight and he had aged years in the span of days. For the first time in my life I saw him cry — tears of joy that he had returned to his family and could see his loved ones again. He told us that he had made my brother pinch him to assure himself that he was still alive.

The new market. The men were held in this church.

Chapter Two

Hardships of Daily Life

A fter this "introduction," the war began to make itself felt in every aspect of our lives.

Long lines formed for bread, which looked and tasted like clay, and there were lines for paraffin, salt, sugar, and soap as well. This last was the first product to disappear from the shops.

The gentiles now came to our soap factory in droves, standing in long lines with pots in their hands. They would snatch from whatever stock was available, not even waiting for it to "gel." Father barely managed store a few boxes for us, so that we might have something to live off for a while. Soap could be exchanged for almost any commodity; the farmers would even give bread and vegetables in exchange for it.

At all events, our factory was completely emptied of soap by the wild crowds, and Father was forced to close permanently.

Later, the Germans came to Father several times to demand soap, and he was forced to give them what he had in the house, but we did manage to store a few bars here and there with friends and relatives, and this reserve helped us later in times of need.

Shopping was no longer something to be taken for granted. Not only did one have to stand in line for hours on end, but in addition the Poles had begun to refuse to sell to Jews. This was not only due to the general shortage, as evidenced by the fact that the bakeries, who received a steady flour ration, also refused to sell to Jews. If a gentile recognized a Jew standing in line, a commotion would start until the Jew would eventually be driven away with shouts and cries and, often, with blows and kicks.

A ration card

My sisters and I would be sent far afield to stand in line for food because, with our fair skins and blonde hair, we did not look particularly Jewish. Nevertheless, it happened many times that after waiting for hours to buy bread, I would reach my turn only to find that the supply had run out. Frustrated, I would have to make my long way home tired and hungry, the more local shops being out-of-bounds due to the danger that I would be recognized as a Jew. We felt clearly that the Germans were not our only enemies. The Poles hated us just as much as they.

At home, too, our lifestyle was much altered. We dismissed our servants, and the burden of the household chores now fell on my mother and on us girls. One Friday, my sisters returned from shopping and told my mother, with a touch of envy, that two of

our neighbors were sitting outside enjoying the sun on the avenue, and they had overheard them saying how lucky they were
that they didn't have to work almost until the onset of Shabbat
like we did.

"My dear daughters," replied Mother, "let us thank Heaven
that we have the means to work for Shabbat. The houses of our
neighbors are empty, and they have nothing to prepare."

These words penetrated my heart and have remained with
me to this very day. On the eve of Shabbat and Jewish holidays,
when I am expecting many guests and have to work late into the
night, I thank God that I have food to prepare — and people for
whom to prepare it....

The curfew, as already mentioned, was in force from 6:00 at
night until 6:00 in the morning. My parents took great care to see
that we were already indoors by 5:30 P.M. To my great joy, I was allowed to subscribe to the local library, although it was expensive,
and the hours of reading during our enforced confinement indoors brought me much satisfaction and contentment.

*   *   *

A terrible fear now seized the Jews of Czenstochow. The Germans proved that they meant business, and anyone so much as
peeping from his window after 6:00 at night was shot. The Germans also confiscated radios and telephones, and new restric-
tions were issued daily, each accompanied by the threat of instant death for anyone who disobeyed:

"It is forbidden to read a newspaper."

"Do not listen to the radio."

"It is forbidden for three people to stand together."

Obviously, the schools were closed, but after several months
of war had passed, during which the children roamed around
with nothing to do and no proper routine, my cousins Reginka
and Madjia began to organize *"kompletim,"* improvised groups of
children of approximately the same age and educational level.
The purpose of these classes was to keep the children occupied

and ensure that they would not be illiterate at the end of the war. Only the most basic subjects were taught. A strict guard was kept throughout, as these groups were conducted against the express orders of the German authorities, and their discovery or exposure would have meant certain death for all concerned. In spite of this, morale was high and we did our best to learn as much as we could, even though we were often hungry.

An underground religious school (*cheder*) was also held. The *melamed* (teacher) was a devout Jew who devotedly preserved his beard, despite the fact that the Germans would forcibly remove the beards of Orthodox Jews by brutally pulling off the hair, often together with the skin beneath it.

All the lessons took place in private homes, and we all hoped that the war would soon end so that we could go back to learning in a normal schoolroom.

The people are being taken from the street to hard labor

Chapter Three

A White Arm Band and a Blue Star of David

After a week of wandering and traveling from place to place, most of our neighbors returned, broken and exhausted in body and spirit. The property that they had left behind them had been stolen and looted, so that even the rich among them were left destitute. My parents did all they could to help these poor souls, and even provided them with linens and blankets.

The month of Elul (August-September), traditionally a time of repentance, drew to a close, and the Jewish High Holy Days approached. It was decided that an improvised synagogue would be set up in the cellar. All the neighbors chipped in and gave whatever they could spare: a table, a chair, or ceremonial objects. My father managed to get hold of a Torah scroll, and the prayers were conducted in the proper manner. Outside the door, people took turns keeping watch, to warn the worshipers if any German approached. We even heard the shofar in the cellar — in shifts!

During the intervening days of the Jewish holiday of Succot, my mother's mother, Grandma Feigele, the daughter of the Rebbe of Piltz (author of *Siftei Tzadik*), died. Grandma Feigele was a pious and intelligent woman. News of her death reached us only when the seven prescribed days of mourning, the *shivah,* were almost over, so that my mother and my uncle sat *shivah* for only one day. My uncle began saying Kaddish three times a day.

One day, the Germans burst into our apartment during prayers and began to search the house. Everyone dispersed except my uncle, who remained standing in prayer, still crowned with his tefillin (phylacteries) and wrapped in his tallit (prayer shawl). He did not move. We all shook with fear. We were sure that the Germans would shoot him on the spot. Instead, a miracle occurred. The German officer ignored the tefillin and tallit, as if he had seen nothing, and at the end of the search he left the house together with his fellow Germans.

The war continued and the Germans demanded the establishment of a "Judenrat," a council of Jewish representatives who would negotiate with them on behalf of the community. More precisely, this meant a group through whom they could transmit their orders to the community. A number of Jews were arrested and held in a cellar without food or water. After two days, they were released and ordered to collect a number of other Jews and to present themselves to the Gestapo within twenty-four hours. This group was then appointed to be the local Judenrat. Although not genuinely representative of our community, the Judenrat did try to work for the benefit of the Jews, and, among other things, it organized *kompletim* to teach sewing to the girls and other skills to the boys. The Germans were aware of these courses but decided, for the time being, to ignore them.

The anti-Jewish decrees grew more and more severe. On the 10th of December, 1939, there came an order that every Jew, male or female, over the age of twelve, must wear a white arm band marked with a blue Star of David on his right arm. Every Jewish shopkeeper was also required to hang in his shop window a blue Star of David on a white ground. These decrees had to be carried out within five days.

Mass production of arm bands began immediately. Some

A pedler with a white arm band and a blue Star of David

were made of cardboard with the star pasted on, while others were made of cloth and required starching and ironing.

These distinguishing marks caused much anxiety within the Jewish community. It was felt that this distinction between Jews and gentiles boded no good.

Another decree, three days later, forbade Jews to travel by bus, train, or other public transportation.

One day, I went for a walk on our avenue. Snowflakes floated in the air and sank slowly to the ground, coating the surroundings in a film of downy whiteness. The trees, the roofs, the benches on the avenue were all clad in white, and against this background the blue Stars of David stood out sharp and clear. I had never before noticed how many Jews lived on Second Avenue, or how many Jewish shops there were.

All these Jews looked worried and anxious, but I could not understand why! Deep in my heart, I felt proud to be a Jew and was sorry that I was not yet twelve years old and old enough to wear the blue and white arm band. I walked up and down the avenue, and in my mind's eye I imagined myself in Israel, in a country where there would be only Jews, and whose symbol would the blue Star of David on a white ground.... However, I kept my fantasies to myself. I would have been laughed at for my naiveté had I told them to others.

On the 24th of December, 1939, at 7:00 in the evening, the big synagogue, which we called the "New Synagogue," was burned, together with all the scrolls inside.

In the meantime, the economic situation worsened and prices rose higher and higher. My mother began to sell some of her valuables in order to provide us with at least one meal a day. She also made great efforts to cook something special for Shabbat. The ingredients could be bought only on the black market.

Then my father came up with the idea of producing a washing powder called "Brilliand" (Diamond), named after the Warsaw soap factory belonging to his brother, which was very well known in those days. He permitted himself to stamp his brother's trademark on the packages of soap powder, which were also sold to gentiles. Obviously, since the production was illegal, he did not print the factory's address.

The new "industry" kept us all busy many hours each day. One of us would mix the ingredients, another would prepare the bags for filling, a third did the actual filling, and the bags were then weighed on scales, which were kept in the bedroom. For many weeks, we were able to breathe more freely. Once more, we could afford enough bread to satisfy our hunger, and sometimes even to supplement this with spread!

For Shabbat, my mother made "gefilte fish" from meat, which tasted like the choicest carp. My father tried to invite guests every Shabbat and extended generous hospitality to them all.

Guests at this time were not hard to find. Refugees streamed from all over the region, and the Jewish population of Czenstochow, which had numbered 25,000 before the war, now swelled to almost 50,000. The refugees were mostly from the surrounding countryside, from neighboring villages and small towns, but some even came from as far away as Lodz.

At this time, about March 1940, the first ghetto was established in Lodz. It existed until its final liquidation in August 1944. People came to Czenstochow thinking that because of its relative smallness, the situation of its Jews might be better. My aunt, Mrs. Vogel, thought so too, and sent her son Chanoch, aged seven, to stay with us until she could manage to reach us with the rest of her family. They planned to save their substantial property for better times. Chanoch quickly got used to us and was soon very much one of the family.

One Shabbat night, as we ate our meal, Chanoch was presented with a full plate of food. At the end of the meal, he was asked if he was satisfied, and he answered: "Well, actually yes, but I'm willing to start all over again from the beginning." And this is perhaps the real meaning of hunger — not to know the meaning of being satisfied...as if the stomach has no bottom.

Chanoch Vogel had two sisters, but nobody from that family survived. When we moved to a two-room apartment in the ghetto, Chanoch was taken by his father's sister, his aunt Polcia. They were all sent to Treblinka.

On the way to Treblinka...

Chapter Four

Typhus

I took ill. My temperature rose and the mercury showed that it was 40° C, continuing to rise to 41° C.

I was burning with fever, and dreamed deliriously of the blue Star of David and Israel. I was unable to eat and could barely swallow liquids. My mother sent for a *felscher* — a sort of superior nurse who, in those days, served also as an unqualified doctor — and he prescribed some unusual medicines and even gave me an injection.

He returned the next day and discovered that my condition had worsened in an alarming manner. Everyone was worried. Through my fever I heard a muffled argument with the *felscher*, who suspected that I had contracted some dreadful disease which he must report to the authorities — at the risk of his own life.

It became clear that I would have to be hospitalized, since my illness was dangerous and contagious. I had contracted typhus.

The following morning, my sister and brother hired a horse and carriage and laid me inside. When the horses broke into a gallop I heard my sister arguing with the coachman, for when he heard our destination, he said, "I'm not going to the hospital for infectious diseases!"

"Why not?" asked my sister, appalled.

"Why not? Here's why not — it's forbidden!"

"If you leave her in the cold street, she'll die."

"If someone finds out that I went to that hospital, they'll confiscate my horse and carriage and I'll die!"

My sister finally brought the conversation to a successful conclusion by "greasing" the man's palm. This convinced him to help us, and he deposited us in the vicinity of the hospital gate, near Chlopickiego Street, and was off like a flash.

My sister took me into the gate of the hospital, where the guard told her to leave me and closed the heavy door on her. For the first time in my life, I was alone. My head was spinning and my knees shook. With great effort I managed to remain standing. After a few minutes a nurse, a nun dressed in black from head to toe, except for a band of white on her veil, approached me, took my hand, and led me off for "treatment."

In the first step of the "treatment," my hair was shaven off and I was bathed. A powerful odor of chlorine and Lysol pervaded the room, and the smell made me even more giddy and confused that I was. The room waved and fluttered before my eyes, and I felt I was drowning. At the end of the "treatment" the nun gave me a thick nightgown made of white cloth like that worn by country folk, and only then was I taken off to bed.

What luxury! I was so happy to be able to lie down in peace. My body burned with fever, I was weak and giddy, and from time to time I was convulsed by waves of shivering. I closed my eyes and was incapable of opening them again. And when I did open them for a fraction of a second, looking down on me from every wall in the room was a crucifix, a wooden crucifix. This was an ironic twist of fate: I was tossed out of my rosy dreams of Israel and Stars of David, into the reality of...crucifixes.

I didn't have the strength to cry or protest. After all, I was only ten years old. I hoped that I would, with God's help, soon be reunited with my parents, but even so, I was grieved at this separation from my beloved family.

When I opened my eyes again, I realized that I was lying in a large room in which there were about forty beds arranged in rows, and in each one a sick woman or girl. I didn't see a single child of my own age. I tried hard to see who my nearest neighbors might be, but didn't have the strength. Once again, my eyes closed, and I slept.

When I awoke again it was already a new day. A nun stood beside me with a glass of tea in her hand. I drank it and began to feel better. My temperature was taken, and the head nurse indicated that the crisis had passed. I would overcome my illness and recover.

Now I could survey my surroundings. All the beds were covered by a simple but clean white cloth. Near each bed was a small night table, painted white. Those girls who were in relatively good condition, and some of the women too, came over to talk to me. They realized I was Jewish and tried to encourage me.

"You are lucky you got over this dangerous illness," they said. "Many die of typhus, and the head nurse told us your condition was very serious; the doctor thought that you would not survive the night."

To my chagrin I also learned that my family would be confined in quarantine for forty days because of me. "All the families (of the sick) are put into a large hall called the *Azil*," they told me, "and there they all stay until each one has suffered the contagious disease and recovered from it." Another woman added: "The whole family gets a space of two square meters, and they all have to shave off their hair."

These tidings were more than I could bear. My beautiful sisters deprived of their hair! All because of me! I was inconsolable. And as if this were not enough, the women told me that the quarantine could last as long as a year, because each member of the family who fell ill added another forty days to the isolation period.

Tears choked my throat, and my heart sank. "Master of the world!" I prayed silently. "Have pity on my beloved parents and

on all our family." I could bear no more. I turned my head away
and blocked my ears.

After several days, I felt better and was able to get up and
walk slowly around the room to seek out acquaintances. Afterwards I went to the window and looked out. The hospital was surrounded by a high barbed wire fence. Visitors stood behind this
fence. I pressed my nose to the glass and, suddenly, I saw my father! I rubbed my eyes and looked again — it was indeed he,
standing among the people, holding a bottle of milk in one hand
and waving his handkerchief with the other. When he recognized me, he smiled.

How wonderful! My father was free and not in quarantine!
My heart filled with new hope and thanks to God for His help.

Later, I learned that the authorities from the Health Bureau
had indeed come to isolate the family for the forty-day required
period. My mother asked my sisters to leave the house so that
they wouldn't be included, but they refused, wanting to be together with their parents in this difficult time. Then the miracle
happened. My cousin happened to know the director of the hospital for infectious diseases personally, and he convinced him to
agree that my family be officially quarantined in their own
home, promising that no one would leave the house during the
prescribed period. Even so, my father came to see me in order to
boost my spirits.

After three weeks, the doctors decided that I was healthy
and could go home. The thought of it filled me with emotion.
How would I be received? How would the children in the *komplet*
regard my shaven head? Would my little brothers recognize me?

My heart beat faster with joy, not unmixed with sorrow
about my naked head.

When I came home, my little brother, Yisroelik, called me "a
boy." "It's not Rutka," he shouted. "It's a boy!"

He was only three and a half years old, but the rejection
pained me. He wouldn't let me hug him. My smiles to him were

in vain. Even my stories could not convince him that it was I, and he kept his distance.

I was sad about my hair, but put on an air of indifference, as if I did not care at all that it had been shaven off. My mother, though, saw through the facade, and one day she said, "Do you know, Rutka, what a person must do to be content? You can be happy under any circumstances, even with a shaven head. It is enough to look around you and see all those who are worse off than you, and then you will always feel that there is room for happiness. Look down, always. That way you will be content and will thank God. There are girls whose homes were looted when their families were sent to the *Azil* for a long time. Their houses were robbed and destroyed, and they had no homes to return to."

This ruse did help me. In all the difficult times I have been through, I always perceived those whose suffering was greater than my own. I learned that both joy and sorrow know no limits and are not subject to absolute laws.

First Avenue, the center of Jewish economic life

Chapter Five

The Establishment of the Great Ghetto

At the end of March, 1940, a new decree was issued: all Jews must leave their homes and move to the ghetto which the Germans had established in the old part of Czenstochow and a few of the surrounding streets. Most of the houses in the old city did not have sanitation, running water, or other basic facilities.

At about this time, the Germans began to remove from Jewish homes any object of value or utility which took their fancy. At first, they "confiscated" this property; later they simplified the process and just took things! Sometimes they would leave a slip of paper which served as a sort of receipt.

To our good fortune, the large poster, saying "Danger" in black letters on a red background, was still pasted to the door of our house since my illness. This frightened the Germans, and for the time being, our property remained in our possession.

Because Second Avenue, where we lived, was not included in the ghetto, we remained in our beautiful home for only a month or so after my return from the hospital. Because our family was highly respected in Czenstochow, the Judenrat gave my sisters a number of addresses in the ghetto, with the permission to choose any apartment they wished. After a long search, my sisters found a fairly comfortable apartment, at least by the standards of those hard times. The apartment was on Krutka Street in a two-story stone building which was divided into two dwellings. Each dwelling had two small rooms and a large kitchen. The wooden floors were painted nut-brown, and the doors and windows were varnished white; everything looked nice and clean.

In the rear courtyard was an outhouse with country-style double sanitary facilities. The house was surrounded by a beautiful garden with a number of fruit trees and a good-sized vegetable garden. Fresh, tall grasses formed a living fence around us, and the whole effect was like a rustic cottage.

In front of the entrance was a small one-story house, also built of stone, separated from our house by a wooden hut, which was also divided into two apartments. The hut had a small courtyard with a well in the middle.

Our new neighbors, who lived on the floor above us, were assimilated Jews who, until their exile to the ghetto, denied their Jewish origin.

The family name was Slonimsky. The brother of our neighbors was the well-known Polish writer Anthony Slonimsky, who was known as a Christian. Our neighbor was the head of a school which held classes even on Shabbat and Jewish holidays, with the weekly day off on Sunday. In spite of this, when the decree banishing the Jews to the ghetto was issued, their Polish neighbors did not hesitate to turn them in to the Germans. They, together with their seventeen-year-old daughter, were forced to uproot themselves from the neighborhood in which they he had lived for so many years and move to the ghetto.

For the first time in their lives, the Slonimskys now saw practicing Jews from close-up, and strictly Orthodox Jews at that. On Friday night, Mrs. Slonimsky, passing our windows, would peep in. When our eyes met, she apologized, "I am sorry for this rudeness, it's just that those candles are so touching."

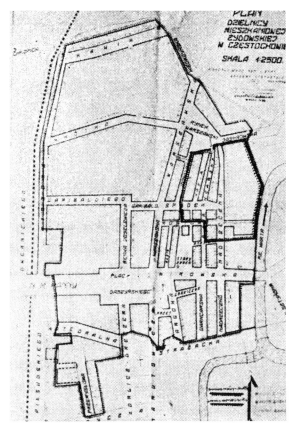

Plan of the ghetto

"That's all right," we answered. "Please come in."

In this way, their interest in the Jewish way of life was aroused, and they were full of astonished questions, like "Why do you check the lentils and throw away the marked ones? After all, the worms are no longer there."

Once, the electricity went out on a Friday night, and we children set up a din in the darkness. Our neighbors, who were used to hearing us sing the Shabbat songs, came down to see what was happening. When they found us sitting in darkness, they ran upstairs and brought us...lit candles.

"No, no, we don't want candles! It's forbidden to light them on Shabbat!"

"But why?" They couldn't understand, and left the candles on the stairs, as our door was open.

*   *   *

Our lives in the new apartment soon settled into a routine. My hair had grown again, and I was able to remove the head scarf from my head. My little brother got used to me again, and, most importantly, our *komplet* reopened in the same place that it had been, on First Avenue, since this was still part of the ghetto. In the *komplet* I studied with my cousin, Marilka, and we were close friends as we were before. We spent many hours together doing homework and reading books. We were twelve and a half years old.

During the time we spent in the ghetto, our economic situation became very difficult. We had to stop producing washing powder because of the crowded conditions in which we lived and also because of the difficulties in marketing it. Jews were allowed to leave the ghetto only by means of a special pass which could be obtained only with great difficulty, and then only by a select few.

My father, who was an honest and straightforward man as well as an expert at his trade, found it hard to tolerate those who produced inferior and cheaper products in times like these. There was a story which he used to tell us about the days of the First World War, but which was applicable to our own times as well. During the war, he said, people used to deal in candles without wicks, in "trousers" with only one leg, in bags of "cocoa" containing ground red brick powder, and so on. When the customer opened his package and found out that his purchase was useless, he would go back to the salesman and complain. However, all he got in response was the retort: "Really, Sir, this product was made to trade in, not to use!"

My father simply could not adapt himself to this kind of thinking.

Chapter Six

The Rebbe of Piltz, Author of "Siftei Tzadik"

Meanwhile, food became more and more scarce.

One day, my father sent me to my cousin to give her something. She received me warmly and offered me supper. I tried to refuse, in order to conceal the extent of my hunger, but the temptation was too much for me.

When I came home, my conscience made me tell my father: "I just couldn't resist. I ate supper at her house."

"Never mind," he answered, smiling sadly, "after all, she is my niece."

*   *   *

My father began to make soap in our kitchen. It was customary to prepare the soap in small portions of up to twenty kilograms. This was no simple matter, but rather involved a great deal of tension, for the Germans and the Polish police would arrest anyone found carrying any kind of parcel, and carefully examine its contents. There was thus a great danger that they would uncover our illegal "factory."

Under these conditions, the major problem was acquiring the raw materials for the soap. This task fell mainly to me, because at this point the Germans were still lenient with small chil-

The Rebbe of Piltz, author of "Siftei Tzadik" ("Lips of the Righteous")

dren. Sometimes my sister would also help. I used to transfer the materials in a little bag which I prepared especially for the purpose.

When the cooking of the soap was completed, it was necessary to cool it, cut it, and weigh it in pieces. When all this was done, the soap was deposited with relatives and friends for storage. Each of them was willing to keep a maximum of two kilos, and therefore my sister and I had to visit a great many families.

Several times, as I left the house with my little package, I would come across a German or Polish policeman. I was very frightened, and I would pray silently to God to help me avoid capture. The family was under great stress until we had gotten rid of our stock. It was in this atmosphere of tension that an accident took place which terrified us all.

My brother, Mendel, had begun to prepare a substance called "calafonia" which was used in the production of our soap. This material was made out of a tree bark and needed to be processed before it was suitable for use. It was highly flammable, and one day indeed caused an outbreak of fire in our house.

We were very frightened. The sight of the flames, and at night too, was likely to arouse the Germans to search for explosives and arrest us all. Desperately, we tried to put out the blaze. We would even have thrown ourselves onto the flames if that would have helped to smother them. In fact, I do not know exactly how we did manage to extinguish the fire — only the Almighty who helped us in our hour of need knows that.

Afterwards, we looked around and surveyed the damage. The kitchen walls and ceiling were begrimed with soot, and the partition and curtains which separated the kitchen from the corridor, forming a small separate room (where my oldest sister and her husband lived), were totally burnt. The damage was extensive, but we were happy nevertheless, because we had not been discovered by the Germans.

Altogether, the word "German" became synonymous with

nightmares and fear, beatings and killings. Our favorable view of the "cultured" Germans had undergone a dramatic change during the occupation.

One evening, my mother, smiling ironically, asked my father, "Do you remember what my grandfather, the Rebbe of Piltz, said about the Germans?"

"Why, yes," recalled Father, "and that was twenty-five years ago!"

"Please tell us," we begged.

So Father related the following story: "Our marriage took place before the outbreak of the First World War, in 1914. My father, your grandfather, Rabbi Josef Dziubas, was the owner of the biggest soap factory of its day in what was then Congress Poland. Prominent among the chassidim of the Rebbe of Gur, he was a rich and aristocratic man and a generous philanthropist, always ready to help others, especially the poor.

"Even the gentiles recognized and acknowledged his goodheartedness. For our wedding, your grandfather furnished our apartment in 38 Second Avenue with the most modern and luxurious furniture from Warsaw. Soon afterwards, the First World War broke out with fighting on two fronts: Germany-Russia and Germany-France. It was a particularly great tragedy for the Jewish people when Jews who were citizens of the three warring states had to fight against their fellow Jews on the "enemy" side. Poland passed from conqueror to conqueror, from the Russian empire to the Austro-Hungarian and German empires.

"When Poland was under German rule, the Jews had good relations with the German Army. At about this time, your mother's grandfather, the Rebbe of Piltz, who was the author of a famous commentary called *Siftei Tzadik* ('The Lips of the Righteous'), came to visit us. We didn't yet have children. Throughout the ten days of his stay, our apartment was filled with Chassidim, his followers and disciples, who came to visit him both by day and by night. When the visit was over, it was hard to discern even the remnants of our home's former luxury — but Mother didn't mind, did you?"

"No. Not at all," whispered my mother. "I was happy to have had the privilege of having so important a man as my guest."

"On the last night of his stay," continued my father, "the conversation turned to the Germans, and your mother grew enthusiastic about them and their civilization, their culture and education, their good manners.... She said, 'They even wash their hands as we do when we invite them to eat.'

"Her grandfather pursed his lips and replied in one sentence: 'Amalek! That's what they are. The real Amalekites — they and their children!'

"Grandfather said no more," concluded my father.

Mother said, "I wondered about his words at the time. I could not understand them at all. But now I do — absolutely."

The tomb of the Rebbe of Piltz (the Siftei Tzadik)

Chapter Seven

Our New Home in the Ghetto

Until the summer of 1942 our lives carried on under relatively tolerable conditions. Although we lived in the ghetto and our movement was restricted, and the burden of providing a living weighed heavily on my parents, they were still able to think of finding a *"shidduch"* — a suitable match — for my sister. It was the third year of the war, and the end was nowhere in sight.

In our crowded apartment we still tried to preserve a certain standard of living. Our room sparkled with cleanliness, and an embroidered cloth, my mother's handiwork, was always spread on the table. Thanks to my recent infectious illness, we still had our own furniture, and our apartment was orderly and well cared for. In the kitchen, the aluminum pots gleamed like mirrors partly because they were now seldom used.

In the corner stood our big copper urn, into which the water that we pumped from the well in the courtyard was filtered. The urn held about three buckets of water. It was so nice to draw water from the little faucet in its side; it was almost like having running water again! My parents had been given this urn as a wedding present, and wherever we lived, they built a special stove for

Shabbat which kept the urn hot from Friday evening at sunset until the end of Shabbat. The water in the urn hummed all Shabbat long, playing a pleasant melody in our ears and in those of the many visitors who came to drink a glass of tea on the day of rest.

The lavatory was in the yard. Once every two months, the wagoner would come by with his long container into which he would empty the contents of the latrines. From there, he would go on to the vegetable fields in nearby villages — this is how they were fertilized. Unpleasant odors wafted from the wagon, and I would hold my breath when it passed.

If we had to use the lavatory at night, we had to go outside to do so. This meant a long and complicated route in the dark, through the young couple's room. Sometimes we preferred to take a shortcut via the window. Only on bitterly cold winter nights did my mother take pity on the little ones and let them use a chamber pot inside the house, lest they catch cold.

Neither was washing as easy as it had been before. We washed once a week in a tub, behind a curtain in the kitchen. When we remembered the beautiful bathroom in our old house on Second Avenue, it was a bit hard to get used to — but we did not complain. Many people were without any kind of roof over their heads at all, and their situation was far worse than ours.

We did a great deal of needlework and sewing. Mother removed the lining and padding from the bedcovers put aside for Pesach and we dyed the cloth, sewed, and embroidered it. We also knitted garments from wool unraveled from old sweaters.

Our sister, who had learnt sewing, sewed us all handsome dresses, skirts, and blouses, each according to her need. Because I had grown taller, I got a new skirt and two blouses — one was even embroidered! When I wore my new clothes, I felt myself, in my mind's eye, to be already grown-up. I was careful not to let anyone feel sorry for me. In the winter, I wore knee socks cut from old stockings. "I'm immune to the cold," I told my friends,

"I simply don't feel it." In order to keep warm, I danced and jumped and acted like a professional sportswoman!

My sister Rivka worked as a bookkeeper in a large company which had a paper factory whose owner and manager was Jewish. The German system of replacing Jewish personnel with gentiles was effectively applied in this factory: they gradually dismissed all the Jewish workers and took over the company themselves. They left the manager in charge until the very last moment. As an expert in his field, he was useful to them.

My brother Mendel was responsible for the vegetable garden. He planted vegetables, and his beetroot, carrots, radishes, and onions contributed substantially to out meager diet. Many times we simply fasted — not, of course, because we wanted to.

As a substitute, we lay on the grass and sunbathed. We didn't want to look pale and feeble. My father would come home, sniffing and smiling. "Something's burning," he would say. But the never-changing beetroot and gruel did not usually burn.

*   *   *

For several weeks we had been getting only a ration of bread — one slice a day. Mother would divide the bread up each morning; it was "dangerous" to leave it in the cupboard, where it might dry up.

One morning, my father sat at the table, which was beautifully spread with a handsome cloth and set with lovely plates, which were almost empty. He washed his hands and recited the blessing over the slice of bread — for even he himself received no more than we children did. While the blessing was still on his lips, there came a knock at the door. My mother opened it and a beggar stood there, looking as if he were about to collapse. Mother handed him a few coppers, but he remained where he was.

"Give me bite to eat," he whispered, "I'm famished...."

When my father heard this, he rose from the table with his own slice of bread in his hand and gave it to the beggar, who hastily snatched it and disappeared from sight.

When the door closed, Mother turned to Father and said, "Why did you do that? That man goes begging from door to door and will certainly get something from somebody or other, while you have given up the only slice of bread you have, and only tomorrow will you get another."

Gently, my father replied, "If everyone thought as you do, that poor man would wear out his legs and fade away with hunger."

In spite of the fact that the feeling of hunger was our constant companion, my sister, my friend and cousin Marilka, and I studied in the *komplet* with some success. We went on to higher classes and learned foreign languages — Latin and German. Marilka even learned a little English and French. Her father, who had returned from abroad at the outbreak of the war, taught her.

Marilka... I still remember her, sitting by my side on the windowsill of her room, enthralled by the story of Helena Mniszek, the first grown-up book we read. The sun was shining from the west and touched Marilka's head with a crown of gold. We tried to cut ourselves off from the bitter reality, at least for a while.

My father would come back from secret meetings with friends, his brow furrowed with wrinkles. The rumors were getting worse, and each day the Nazis devised some new, harsher decree against the Jews.

In the villages and hamlets around Czenstochow, the Germans turned the Jews out of their homes and expropriated their property. Jews from the Lodz ghetto were being sent to labor camps, and rumors began to seep through that the Germans had started mass deportations to labor camps. Some said that only men were being sent, others that the deportations included women, but without their children.

Refugees were streaming in from all directions. Each large family was allotted a room by the community. Everyone tried to help them as much as they could. Conditions were very difficult, with sometimes as many as twelve persons crammed into one room. Mother collected garments we had outgrown; she repaired, washed, and ironed them and gave them to refugee families. She also gave them furniture and household goods. Despite the shortage of food, she would send special dishes for Shabbat to some distinguished widows who had come down in the world. She did not entrust this task to any of the children. She herself would go to these women with her gifts, prompted by the noble and refined spirit which was her trademark.

Immediately after lighting the Shabbat candles, Mother, weighed down by a bag full of loaded containers and jars, would set off. This bag was kept for mitzvot.

My father encouraged this activity. He said that in times of trouble Jews should go out of their way to help each other, and in this way we would bring the Day of Redemption closer.

Altogether, Father did not lose his good spirits or his firm belief in God. As a rich man and an aristocrat by birth, he probably suffered more than most, but he never complained. He was an aristocrat even without his property. I came to understand that people can be poor in spirit, despite great wealth, while others, who lack everything, are actually rich, because real wealth is not measured in possessions but in the essence of one's deeds and in greatness of spirit.

Kidnapped Jews, sent to forced labor

Chapter Eight

The Noose Tightens

Help yourself, Rutka," Marilka's mother handed me a slice of bread and jam.

"No, thank you." I swallowed hard. "I've just had lunch."

How good the smell of that bread was! How fresh and soft, how appetizing — and how lucky that my poor stomach was not transparent! I was so embarrassed to admit that I was starving, yet after a couple of hours, my resistance weakened. I surrendered to Marilka's mother and took the slice of bread she offered. It tasted wonderful. I chewed it slowly so that I would not miss a moment of the treat — and so that my cousin should not realize how hungry I was.

Today, most people take food for granted and don't know how to appreciate the feeling of being satisfied.

The unfortunate refugees were grateful for every mouthful of food. At daybreak they would stand in long lines, pots in hand, in order to get their daily ration from the soup kitchen which the Judenrat had set up. The lines got longer and longer each day, and there was soon concern that there would not be enough soup to go around.

This was the situation at the beginning of autumn, 1942. The High Holy Days were approaching and with them, the signs of fall. The leaves fell from the trees and were carried here and there by the wind. "Like refugees," I thought. "Like human beings caught up in the toils of war." Even the heavens were grim and grey, though small strips of blue still peeked out here and there from among the ragged clouds.

It was then that my Grandmother Dziubas, my father's mother, died quietly in her sleep. She was ninety-eight years old and had been widowed in 1938. Since the death of my grandfather, she had lived with her daughter. We grandchildren would visit her from time to time, and she always received us kindly, telling us stories and giving us sweets. We loved our grandmother, a warmhearted person who helped everyone. She had cared for Grandfather's workers like a mother, herself baking cakes for their weddings and providing each one with a generous dowry, all with Grandfather's approval and encouragement.

My father used to visit her every day, even when there was curfew. Now he quietly wept for her. When someone remarked that his mother had been granted a long life and had enjoyed much gratification from her children, Father replied, "But she was my mother — and a mother is ageless."

About thirty people accompanied my grandmother to her rest, and we had a special permit enabling us to hold a funeral service. She was laid alongside my grandfather, whose grave was close to my mother's grandfather, the author of *Siftei Tzadik,* in the Chassidic section of the Czenstochow cemetery. As early as 1943, the Italian marble headstones were taken by the Germans to the Hasag factory, but small plaques identifying the graves did remain, and after the war my brother-in-law located the three tombs and fenced them off.

Heaven was merciful to my grandmother, and she was taken before the situation became unbearable.

The New Year's prayers, coming shortly after Grandmother's death, were held in an atmosphere of increasing gloom and despondency. The prayers took place in a hut near our house, and all the residents of Krutka Street gathered there. Sad rumors circulated. In a nearby village, five Jews had been hanged. Someone remarked with bitter irony that this was a good sign — perhaps the Germans were running out of ammunition.

Until the middle of 1942, no news of what was happening in occupied Poland reached the outside world. Those reports which did filter through were discredited as exaggerated. In August, 1942, Dr. Riegner of the Jewish Agency sent a cable to the Allied High Command in which he warned that, according to secret information which he had received from an informant known to have connections with high-ranking Nazi officers, a "final solution" to the problem of Poland's three and a half million unwanted Jews was being planned, using the poison gas Cyclon-B. However, Riegner himself wrote that although reports from that source were usually reliable, he himself doubted the veracity of the information.

In June of 1942, a cry for help was cabled from the Underground Resistance in the Warsaw ghetto begging the free world to open its eyes and realize that genocide was being committed, with the Jews of Europe as the victims.

At that time, before the machinery of extermination and death was fully set in motion, it might still have been possible to save the Jews. But nothing was done.

The Allies claimed that they were fighting against German control on a universal scale, and that their fight was against the Nazi regime as a whole. Even Winston Churchill, who well understood the full extent of what was happening, did not use the full weight of his authority and influence on his colleagues to persuade them to act on the matter. Apparently, the Jewish victims were not sufficiently important to the Allied High Command, and they did not realize that by saving the Jews, they would be helping their own cause.

In the meantime, rumors of the forthcoming deportation of the Czenstochow community grew. In spite of this, my father would not leave the town where three generations of his family had lived. The family had been well liked and well respected by the townspeople, and my father hoped that perhaps some of the Christians would recall bygone days and would lend us a helping hand.

On the Day of Atonement, the holiest day of the Jewish year, tension increased and there were reports that the "Black Hats" — the Ukrainians — had arrived. These Ukrainians were known to be the collaborators of the Germans, and they carried out with speed and fidelity the diabolical plans of their masters. There was talk of an immediate deportation — of an *aktion.*

During the day, I went for a walk in the ghetto with my friend Liptzia from the *komplet.* As we walked she taught me a pretty little song about childhood, which passes so swiftly. Was our childhood already passing? Was it already over? After all, we were thirteen years old.

We walked along Wilson Street until we reached Second Avenue, which was, of course, outside the ghetto. Suddenly, we were confronted with a large poster affixed to a wooden board, stating in large black letters in Polish and German: "No thoroughfare for Jews. Trespassers will be shot on sight."

The pleasure of our walk faded for us. We separated and returned home with a feeling of impending disaster in our hearts. I felt that my parents, my older brother, and my sisters were also deeply worried. We did not talk about it, but each of us felt the anxiety and dread of the next. It was evening on the Day of Atonement; the Gates of Heaven were still open to our prayers.

With the ending of the Holy Day, Father rapidly said Havdalah and a deep sadness filled his eyes. Apparently, he knew more than we did about preparations for the *aktion.* At the festive meal breaking our day of fasting, we could not bring ourselves to eat a morsel.

"Put the children to bed in their clothes," said Father quietly.

I realized that I had not been included in his command, and I felt suddenly that, indeed, I had grown up.

Chapter Nine

The Aktion

O ur house was alive with alert activity that night. Father, grave and anxious as we had never seen him before, went in and out, with neighbors in his wake, talking in whispers with a strange and frightening secrecy. They decided that everyone should go down to the cellar that very same night.

"Take down two beds, two buckets of water, and one bucket for a latrine," my father instructed my brother and brother-in-law. My mother wrapped a few loaves of bread in a napkin, woke my younger brothers, and we all went down to the cellar.

This cellar was under the hut next door to our house, where the Kolin family lived. In the "bunker," we now numbered fifteen souls. We ourselves were eleven — eight children, my parents, and my brother-in-law. Mr. Kolin and his wife made two more, and Mrs. Goldman and her daughter completed the count. Mrs. Goldman was a widow who lived in a large house opposite our own. She happened to visit us at the end of Yom Kippur and, overhearing talk about the bunker, had asked my father to shelter her, which he agreed to do.

Towards morning, we managed to finally settle inside. Suddenly, someone knocked on the door: "Have pity on my wife and three small children," he begged. "On Garibaldi Street they have already received notice of the *aktion* and everyone — men, women, and children — have been ordered to leave their homes

In the small hours of the night we managed

to settle inside, in the bunker

and gather in the New Market. The Germans are allowing people to take only a few possessions. They have warned that anyone found in his home after 9:00 in the morning will be shot on sight."

Each person was allowed to take only a few things with him, and people simply did not know what to choose. Some only carried their children, others took their tallit and tefillin, still others, their gold and jewelry.

Despite our own desperate overcrowding, my father could not turn these people away. "God will help us all," he said, hoping that the difficult hours would pass quickly. In the morning, Mr. Kolin's married son, who lived in another neighborhood, arrived and reported that the *aktion* had started, along with deportations from the town. When he left, he disguised the entrance to our bunker with lengths of wood, like floorboards. On top of this he loaded boxes of bottles, and on top of these he sprinkled sand, so that they would look as if they had been there for some time.

My mother and we children were "settled" on the two beds. The Kolins sat on a mattress with Mrs. Goldman and her daughter, while my father, my brother Mendel, and my brother-in-law sat on the floor, together with the family that had joined us. My father asked us all to refrain from speaking in order to conserve, as much as possible, the small supply of oxygen in the bunker. In spite of this restriction, within only a few hours we began to feel a sense of suffocation; twenty people were breathing in the air in that tiny, closed space. The candle my brother had lit flickered and went out at once. We felt that we, too, would not be able to hold out for very long. Mrs. Kolin fainted, as did Mrs. Goldman, and we felt the world around us begin to blur and fade.

My father and brother tried to lift the hatch over the bunker, but did not succeed. Young Mr. Kolin had done his work well, assuming that the *aktion* would last for only a few hours and that thereafter, he himself would come back to release us.

My father became weak and my brother began to breathe

*In the dead of the night we left the bunker, my father and I, to
draw water from the well in the yard.*

heavily. They gathered their strength and prayed to God to help them, if only for a moment, as he had helped Samson the hero in his hour of need. Then they tried once more to move the coverings. Sweat ran down my brother's face and even with his young years and sturdy build, he had great difficulty in shifting the load of heavy wooden boards and boxes of bottles. He struggled desperately until, suddenly, the boards creaked and a stream of fresh air penetrated our lungs. God, ever loving and merciful, had not abandoned us in our distress.

*   *   *

Only three days later did young Mr. Kolin return. He bore news of the *aktion* which was still going on, street by street. He told us that he hoped it would end within a few days. He suggested that my brother and brother-in-law leave the bunker. "The Germans need healthy young men to work, and so they will have a good chance of remaining in Czenstochow, and alive," he explained. Besides, once outside, it would be easier to keep track of what was going on and to decide when to release the family from the bunker.

My brother Mendel and my brother-in-law, with Father's agreement, took their leave of us all, and especially of my father, with mixed emotions.

In the meantime, the supply of food had dwindled, despite the care we exercised in rationing out bread and water. After a few days, the water supply was depleted and not even a crumb of bread remained. I remembered with longing the food I had left on the table after Yom Kippur. If only I were able, now, to bite into one potato.

Father, the instinctive leader of our group, realized that we could not survive without water and that we must take steps to ensure that we would have a supply: "Who will come with me to fetch some water?" he asked. No one answered. We all sat without moving, numb with fear. Any peep outside was likely to mean a death sentence. Then I, the little one, got up and volunteered to go with him.

In the dead of night we left the bunker, my father and I, to draw water from the well in the yard. How good it was to breathe the fresh air! The heavens were clear, sprinkled with silver stars, and a light breeze stroked our faces and played a wonderful melody in the branches of the trees. No human voice disturbed the harmony of this scene, no footsteps, no creaking carts, no snorting horses. In the whole of the great ghetto, there was only my father and I, together in the heart of nature, protected by God in heaven.

We lowered the bucket down with the winch and it rubbed against the sides of the well. Its banging sounded deafening to our ears. We held our breath and waited tensely, clutching the bucket of water without moving. Only after some time, when no German or Pole hailed us, did we breathe freely again. Cautiously, we took hold of the bucket and brought it back to the bunker, where the others were waiting anxiously.

People praying in a bunker

Chapter Ten

In the Bunker

The next day. It was already light outside, but in the bunker we could not distinguish night from day. Suddenly we heard a noise as if something was being scraped over the ground. We pricked up our ears, and the scraping was heard again.

We realized that someone was at the hatch, removing the layer of earth which my father and Mr. Kolin had spread over us to disguise the entrance to the bunker.

A tense silence reigned in the cellar. All hearts beat rapidly. In the complete darkness all our eyes turned towards the hatch. Suddenly a ray of light pierced the bunker and blinded our eyes, which had not seen light for over ten days and were now accustomed to the darkness. The crack in the hatch widened and with it, the light. With growing fear we waited for what was to come.

"Are you alive?" called out the dear familiar voice of my brother Mendel. We could not utter a sound in answer, but a movement or noise must have reassured him.

"We'll soon get you out of here. We were thinking about you all the time!" he added.

A minute later, three bottles of water and some pieces of dry bread were let down into the bunker by a rope.

"We are alive," someone managed to answer in a feeble voice, and upon hearing that my brother hastened to cover the hatch with earth and disappear as if he had never been. My father, who at that moment had been in a small corridor above the bunker saying the morning prayers, was very disappointed. He had so longed to see his son and hear his voice...but the opportunity was missed.

My brother's fate was sealed in the selection which took place near our home on Krutka Street. A German by the name Dagenhardt stood there with a small stick in his hand, calling out "left" or "right" to each person who passed before him. A number of other Nazis stood around to assist him. None of the young people who were the objects of the selection knew that those words which the German called out really meant "life" and "death." Nor did they know which side was the "good one." My brother was sent to the left, my brother-in-law to the right. And that is how each one saw the other for the last time.

The group sent to the left, which included my brother, was marched to the train station and put into boxcars, which took them straight to Treblinka. My brother-in-law, together with a small group of other men, was sent to forced labor.

*   *   *

Meanwhile, in the bunker, another three days passed without any contact with the outside world. The bread and water that my brother had brought us ran out: eighteen people had partaken of them. Again, an argument broke out regarding our seemingly hopeless situation.

"Why are we hiding?" my sisters asked my father. "We can't stay alive without food and water."

"If we go out," answered my father, "we'll be deported."

"So what? What's so terrible about that?" insisted my sisters. "We can live somewhere else, and manage just as others do. When the war ends we can go home again."

It never occurred to us that the deportations meant Treblinka and the gas chambers. But Father insisted that we remain where we were.

I lifted my gaze and behold, the tip of a rifle bar

hed   through the curtains, black and glistening

The next night, Father and I went out of the bunker once more, this time to the garden next to our house. Our neighbors, we knew, had tomato plants. They had probably not had time to pick them all, and perhaps we would find some which were ripe for eating.

We took a basket and began, by moonlight, to pick everything that came to hand. Not only were there tomatoes, but also cucumbers, spring onions, and radishes. I will never forget the sweet taste of those firm green tomatoes. To my stunned and empty stomach, they were a delicacy.

Four more days passed. Young Mr. Kolin stopped coming. There was no sign of life from Mendel or my brother-in-law. We were despondent. Everyone was depressed, almost despairing. We thought our lives would end in that sealed bunker.

Only Father was filled with faith and hope. He did not cease to anticipate God's salvation, which would surely come.

He gathered all his ingenuity to find a solution, even a temporary one, to our situation. Then an idea occurred to him, and he explained to me: "You know, my friend Reizman's factory is close to our house. I have heard that there are Jews working there for the Germans and that they eat and sleep on the premises. We can assume that smoke, therefore, comes out of the factory chimney. So we, too, will light our stove."

I tried to follow his reasoning.

"We will light the stove? In our house?"

"Look," said Father patiently. "According to my calculations, if we go to the house and light the stove, you can cook something with some of the flour we have stored there and no one will notice that the smoke is coming from our house and not from the factory. What do you say?"

My older sisters were simply too terrified to help, and my mother had to stay in the bunker to keep the little ones calm and quiet. Of course, I agreed to go with my father. In the middle of the day, we set off with beating hearts, like thieves in the night.

My father carried out the complicated task of lighting the stove and then left me alone to "cook." He had to return as quickly as possible to his charges in the bunker.

I found some flour in the kitchen cupboard and decided to make dumplings. My culinary knowledge was somewhat sketchy, to say the least. I had never taken an interest in the subject, and my mother had thought me too young to learn. Now I was entrusted with the task of cooking for our "family" in the bunker.

Full of good intentions, I put a large pot of water on the fire that Father had lit. I mixed the flour with water and formed the dumplings. The water was not even boiling when I put the dumplings into the pot, and they immediately congealed into a dark, sticky mess.

"Never mind," I said to myself. "As soon as the water boils the 'food' will cook."

The water had been standing in our house for several weeks, and I had learned in my biology lessons that bacterial cultures form in water. Now I recalled these lessons. "I hope they don't get sick from this dish," I thought.

While I waited for the water to boil, I used the time to tour the house. I breathed the sweet air with pleasure and soaked in the daylight which was absent from the bunker. In the dining room was a long table. On a pristine tablecloth were laid fine cutlery and the plates from our best dinner service, which still contained those potatoes, now rotten with mildew — all that was left of the meal following the Day of Atonement fast. I stood looking at them and again asked myself how I could have left such dainties without eating them.

I shook myself uneasily. If I were discovered here I was lost. I returned to the kitchen and lifted the lid of the pot to see if the water had boiled. At that moment I heard a slight rustling. I lifted my gaze and, behold, the tip of a rifle barrel reached through the curtains, black and glistening. My knees shook and prickled. "All is lost," I thought. "This is the end."

Chapter Eleven

By the Skin of Our Teeth

A Polish policeman in all his splendor stood before me, a large gun over his shoulder.

"What are you doing here, girl? For whom are you cooking? Where are the Jews hiding?"

While he was still spraying me with questions, I thought quickly and resolved: "I won't give away the hiding place. Come what may — I'll save my parents and my dear family from death." I repeated this over and over again. "Anyway, I'm done for."

I drew myself up and said, "I'm all alone here. I'm hiding alone in this house."

"Where are the others?" said the policeman. "You'll never make me believe that all that food is just for you!"

Stubbornly, I repeated my reply with emphasis: "I'm all alone here and I have prepared this food to feed myself over the next two weeks."

"God," I prayed, "don't let my family be discovered."

The policeman stared searchingly at me. I didn't move, preparing myself inwardly for the blows I felt sure were to come. I was prepared for anything — except that the bunker be exposed.

As we stood facing each other, there came to my ears the sound of soft footsteps: "Another policeman," I thought. But to my great astonishment, I saw my father appear. He went up to the policeman and said firmly, "I said that I would give you the jewelry, only if you promise to keep our secret."

I looked wonderingly from one to the other. The policeman gave his word not to betray us, and my father pointed to a small bundle lying near the well. In this bundle were wrapped the gold jewelry of all the people in the bunker. The policeman left the house, picked up the parcel, and left as he had come.

With the large pot in my trembling hands, and with my father's help, we went back to the bunker. It became clear that someone had found a slice of bread, and a loud argument had broken out among the starved inhabitants of the bunker. The policeman, passing through the ghetto, had heard the raised voices and knocked on the door of the hut. All became silent at once, but my father, who was brave, noted that the knocking was softer than was characteristic of the Germans.

"Maybe it's a Jew in need of help," thought Father, "and we must save him." He went to the door, opened it — and recoiled; an armed Polish policeman stood facing him.

"Give me your gold jewelry!" demanded the Pole from my bewildered Father.

"We will give you everything we have," replied Father, "but only on the condition that you don't turn us in."

At all events, the policeman had decided to take a look inside the house as well, where he found me. He evidently thought I belonged to a different bunker and that he might manage to extort something from this second group as well.

My mother took the pot from us and dished out a hot meal to everyone. The pot held enough food for another day, perhaps even two. But it was emptied that same evening — so thoroughly that we didn't even have to clean it.

Again, days and nights went by, indistinguishable one from another, and the bunker was bare of food once more. None of those who had promised to help had returned. Since we did not doubt their good intentions, this gave us all the more reason for worry and anxiety.

Our lives were totally cut off from reality, devoid of any information from the outside and empty of hope. Once again, Father was the one who reminded us that even with a sword at his throat, a man must not despair of Heavenly mercy. One must never lose faith.

Nonetheless, our serious situation required some kind of remedy. Father went up to the storeroom above the bunker and sat there alone, trying to work out a solution. Then an idea came to him. We could look for food in the abandoned house across the road.

We knew that other people had done this in our house. At night we heard them going inside, taking clothes, bedding, warm blankets, and food. We could not protest; we didn't want them to discover our hiding place. And now, Father decided, it was permissible to take food from other abandoned homes since it was definitely a matter of life and death.

As soon as he had decided upon this course of action, Father suggested to me and David, the thirteen-year-old boy whose family had joined us in the bunker the day after Yom Kippur, that we be the ones to go on this great mission. David and I both agreed.

It was impossible for my father to have gone himself, for his responsibility to the people in the bunker required that he be there at all times. In the dark, the twenty starving, frightened people would certainly have quarreled or panicked, and the noise would have endangered the entire bunker. He had no choice but to send us children.

Our destination was a large three-story house opposite our own. Each of us took two baskets, and in the middle of the night we left the bunker. It was November of 1942, and we could feel the autumn chill in the air. David and I crossed the road a few minutes apart. I went first and waited in the shelter of the doorway.

"It doesn't make sense for both of us to look in the same

apartment," I told him. "I'll take the upper floors, you take the lower."

"All right," he agreed.

"We'll meet in one hour on the second floor — all right?"

"Good."

The house was pitch dark. The apartments were strange, and it was hard to find the kitchen. The doors and windows were wide open, and the wind roared through the house, unobstructed. Bottles and jars gave off strange, weird sounds. The open windows rattled loudly and the roof creaked. I stood in that mysterious and frightening room, and suddenly froze in terror; something gleamed in the corner! I forced myself to approach — and almost wept with relief. An abandoned and frightened cat stood there motionless. Was she also hungry? Was she dying here in the dark?

People arriving to Treblinka

The big house on Krutka Street, from which we took food to the bunker

Chapter Twelve

Terror in the Dark

In that dark house, full of whispers, I groped in the thick blackness. In my hand I held the box of matches that my father had given me for emergency use only. I wished with all my heart to banish the darkness, just for an instant, but I dared not, for fear that the small spark of light would give me away.

Step by step, I felt my way along the walls, until at last I found the kitchen. A row of cabinets containing various staples gladdened my heart. For an hour, I filled my basket while every banging door made me jump and the creaking windows sent my heart into my boots.

With how many voices does an empty house speak; a mournful language of loss and desolation....

On the second floor I met David, who also had a full basket in his hand.

"Let's go back to the bunker," we decided, "and come back again in a few days. There's surely what to come back for, but for now, it's enough."

The darkness, the strange noises, and the whistling wind scared and depressed me. We had to leave.

We stood in the doorway, our baskets in hand — but we could not cross the road. The peace of the night was deceiving. Once, human voices disturbed the silence, once the creak of boots. As I tried for the third time to cross the road, I heard voices

The frightened people were guarded by the gestapo on both sides.

from afar. This, too, was a warning signal for us.

I do not know how long we stood there in the dark, on that starless night, waiting. We saw how the dark of night gradually withdrew and how lightly the cloak of darkness lay upon us. This time, we decided, there was no choice, we had to cross.

"God will help us," I said in a whisper.

Hastily, I crossed the road, and after a little while, David followed me. We went into the bunker with the heavy baskets in our hands and were received with open arms. My mother and father, filled with worry, had not been able to sleep and had stood all the while at the door of the bunker waiting for us. My father kissed my head and praised me warmly. "Your courage has saved us all from death by starvation."

My heart swelled to hear these words from my father. It was worth suffering even such an ordeal of terror, to hear Father say such nice things.

*   *   *

Within a week, our supplies were depleted. It was time for another sortie. This time, we equipped ourselves with sacks. We even planned a visit to the bakery across the road. Perhaps we would find flour there, or bread from before the *aktion*; it was a Jewish bakery whose proprietors had been deported without any advance warning.

I was also entrusted with an additional mission. Mrs. Goldman, who had lived in the large house from which we had brought the food previously, asked me to bring her heavy gold chain which she had left behind.

"It weighs 250 grams," she apologized. "That's why I'm asking you. Who knows, perhaps we shall be saved, my daughter Chava and I, through this necklace?"

With explicit directions as to the exact location of the chain, we set off once again. This time we went just before dawn, when the darkness was lifting somewhat. This way, we would be able to see better and wouldn't need to grope in the darkness. We waited,

Forced labour march

pricking up our ears; were those suspicious voices?

Yes. Voices and the sound of footsteps — but not the evil echo of jackboots, only the tired tread of people marching. Many footsteps from many feet.

I looked at David; his face was pale. I signaled to him with my hand and whispered, "Follow me."

Unhesitatingly, we broke into an apartment in the little house by the side of the road. We climbed into the unmade beds that had been left here.

The footsteps came nearer, and we heard words in Yiddish and Polish, followed by shouts in German: "Quicker! Move it! Tempo!"

I peeped out from under the blanket and through the windows saw thousands of people, some with children in their arms, all with bundles on their backs, their provisions for the journey. The procession went on and on, the frightened people guarded on both sides by the Gestapo. These had loaded rifles in their hands, and from time to time they used them to land cruel blows on the backs of anyone who held them up or delayed them even

The railway station in Czenstochow

a little bit. I couldn't tell if the marchers were from Czenstochow or not. I crawled back under the blanket, trembling in fright. Where were they taking these people and their children? Where were they all going?

Later I learned that these people were taken to the railway station of Czenstochow. After each "selection," thousands were sent by train to the death camp in Treblinka.

*   *   *

After a long while, everything was silent again. The street lay quiet and no living soul was to be seen.

We went back outside and checked out the area. When I was convinced that all was clear, I crossed the road. The eight meters of its width seemed to me as wide as the ocean. We had to take so many steps to cross it....

We arrived. I parted from David, and this time he searched the upper floors while I went to Mrs. Goldman's apartment and to the bakery.

"We'll meet in about an hour?"

"Yes, near the gate of the big house."

"Good luck!"

The selection

I peeked out and saw thousands of people with children in their arms and bundles on their backs.

Chapter Thirteen

In the Bakery

I started off by looking for the gold chain in Mrs. Goldman's apartment. According to her instructions, there was a loose tile in the kitchen. "The fifth tile on the left beyond the wall cupboard," I repeated to myself. But the panic which almost overwhelmed me made me forget some of the directions, and I had to search long and hard until, at last, I found it.

I then decided to go to the bakery, which was in a large yard surrounded by a simple wooden fence. I reached the yard at a run, and I looked for the best place to seek the bread.

Suddenly I heard someone shout in German, "Here's the bakery!" The heavy steps of boots accompanied the shout. I had to find a hiding place immediately. My eye fell on a large dough-mixer, and without a moment's hesitation I jumped inside.

Seconds later, three Germans came into the bakery and began strolling about, as if it belonged to them. They began to count the sacks of flour and to list their numbers, and wandered all over the place contentedly, as if it had always been theirs. I shut my eyes and held my breath. My heart beat furiously, and I thought that the Germans would surely hear its pounding.... I knew that if they discovered me they would shoot me without mercy, as they would a dog. The Nazis were devoid of any human feeling. One of them leaned against the mixer and began tapping a rhythm on its side with his stick. With every tap, I feared he would pierce my heart. To my good fortune, it seems that this particular German was not very musical, as he did not notice that the sound he made was not that which should have resounded from a hollow vessel!

It grew later and later. Every second seemed like an hour, and I felt that my lungs would burst. I turned my thoughts to our Father in Heaven and prayed silently: "Merciful One, please save me from these murderers... only You can help me now!"

*   *   *

After about a quarter of an hour, which seemed to me immeasurably long, I heard one of them say, "Let's go now."

Once again, the sound of heavy boots, this time fading into the distance.

I was saved! God in Heaven had heard my cry and saved me. I breathed deeply, filling my lungs with air. Slowly, slowly, my breathing returned to normal.

I hopped out of the mixer and got myself together. I shook out my sack and filled it with everything I could lay my hands on.

Now that the danger had passed, I was bathed in a cold sweat. My floury white hands shook violently. All I wanted to do was to go back immediately, to the bunker and my loving parents. I badly needed their soothing presence and warmth. I gathered my strength and crept up to the gate of the big house, where David was already waiting with two full sacks in his hands. One was full of food, and the other was full of all kinds of valuables — suits, jackets, and silverware. He had taken the extra sack secretly, intending to fill it with these items.

We returned safely with our sacks. On the way, David said to me, "You're a fool, Rutka."

"Me?" I asked in confusion. "Why am I a fool?"

"You risked your life — and for what?"

"What do you mean, 'for what'?" I replied, stunned. "The bread..."

"I don't mean the bread," he interrupted. "I mean the chain! In my opinion, it should belong to you."

"But it belongs to Mrs. Goldman!"

"True, but you endangered yourself for it, and she would never have done so. She would never have endangered her Chava like that. Maybe you could also someday save yourself with the chain — and maybe even help your loved ones."

This reasoning seemed to make some sense, and therefore I did not answer Mrs. Goldman when she asked if the chain had been found. I drew my father aside, told him what David had said, and asked, "Was he right?"

"Heaven forbid!" interrupted Father. "How could you even think of such a thing! The chain is not yours!"

I was ashamed and immediately handed over the chain. Deep down, I felt proud of my father, who even under those dehumanizing conditions was not tempted, even for a moment, to stray one hairsbreadth from the path of honesty and truth.

He was angry with David because he had stolen other people's property, and rebuked him, saying, "These items are not a matter of life or death. We have no right to take anything but food."

"In these times, everything is considered ownerless," argued David, "and ownerless property, one is permitted to take."

*   *   *

Another week dragged by in the bunker, and once again our supply of food ran out. During the five weeks that we spent in that cramped space, we had not washed, and we felt filthy. "What will happen?" we asked ourselves incessantly. "Are we doomed to be buried here? Is there any chance of being saved? How will we continue to get food and water?"

Once again, it was my father who did not despair. He allowed himself to think only in a productive manner. This time, his idea was centered around the Reizman factory, next to our house. Father figured that, although the Germans generally ap-

pointed their own supervisors (*kommissars*) to be in charge of
Jewish factories, Mr. Reizman had probably remained in the factory. Perhaps he still had some influence. If we sent him two girls
with a request for help, he would certainly do all he could to help
us. My mother also agreed that we had to make contact with the
outside world, as we could not stay in the bunker indefinitely.
The next morning, it was decided, Hela and Rivka would set out
on this great mission.

These people and their children are being taking to selection

Chapter Fourteen

My Sisters

So, that's settled," concluded my sisters. "Tomorrow evening we'll contact you in some way, and we'll try to send you some food."

"Don't forget to write in detail how you are doing," added Father.

The same morning that my sisters left, we heard heartrending cries and screams from the direction of the factory. The cries of adults and children blended with the terrible shouts of the Germans and the barking of dogs. Our hearts froze in terror; we understood that something dreadful was happening there. We realized that a "selection" was going on and that, in the searches, bunkers with children and old people had been disclosed.

This awful day at last ended, and night fell. At the appointed hour, I went out with my father to the rendezvous; this was in the next courtyard where a garden with a wall, about twelve feet high, separated our house from the Reizman factory. Near the top of the wall was a narrow crevice through which one could pass objects or exchange things.

We stood near this opening and waited. After a while, we heard a whispered call from my sisters on the other side. My father replied, and they began to slip a few radishes and carrots through the slit in the wall. Finally, down fluttered a letter. I bent down to retrieve the vegetables and the letter, and a giant radish suddenly landed on my head. It was a large one, weighing over two pounds, and in proportion to its size was the shock which came over me. Even so, I was happy, as we now had something to eat!

Suddenly I noticed that the moon and stars were lighting up the night sky, and with an uplifted face I thanked God for his goodness. How beautiful were the dark blue heavens! The large round moon shone like silver, while all around the stars sparkled. The trees in the garden rustled their scant branches, and from time to time another leaf would fall to the ground. It could no longer manage to cling to its tree, poor thing.

This was already the end of November, the middle of autumn. Father opened the note and began reading by the light of the moon while I tried to "hoard" a supply of fresh air in my lungs. While we were still standing there, we heard names being called; a roll call was going on in the factory. At that moment, I envied those people, marked down on the "list of the living," with all my heart.

At the same moment, thoughts passed through my mind, which one usually doesn't delve into too deeply. "How should a person feel, who has been granted permission to live? A person who is allowed to breathe, to drink as much water as he desires?" These are rights which people take for granted, seemingly simple things which they do not know how to appreciate.

In the bunker, they were waiting for us anxiously. The hands of the clock had moved slowly for them; our short trip had seemed to them very long, and they worried about us and my sisters. They waited eagerly to hear what had happened that day at the factory.

We understood that in all probability, our own future depended on the answer to this question.

*   *   *

Father spread out the letter and read it aloud, while we hung on his every word.

"This very morning," wrote my sisters, "the Germans arrived suddenly with tracer dogs and carried out a selection. Everyone was ordered to go out into the big courtyard, and a list of workers was read out. Whoever was not listed was ordered to stand aside and was deported. This inspection was not enough, however, and the dogs were ordered to seek out those in hiding. The well-trained dogs found bunkers on the territory of the factory where Mr. Reizman's parents, his small children, and other members of his family were hiding. Children were bitten by the dogs, and their clothing was left hanging in the beasts' jaws. The Germans shot children before the very eyes of their despondent parents. It was a dreadful, nightmarish scene. Everyone was shaking with fear and stood by helplessly. When some of the mothers ran towards their children, the Germans drove them back with murderous blows.

"Later, any 'illegals' who remained alive were taken to the railway station. Here, boxcars awaited them.... These were the boxcars which took them to the death camps."

My sisters wrote that "Mr. Reizman had received (them) kindly." Fortunately, they had arrived two hours before the selection, and Mr. Reizman had told the *kommissar* of the factory about them. This man was an "ethnic German" — a Pole of German extraction. Mr. Reizman said, "These girls are the daughters of my friend Mr. Dziubas, and this is a matter of life and death. He begs that we save them."

"Dziubas," said the *kommissar*. "Why, my father was the manager of his soap factory." (He meant my grandfather, Josef Dziubas). The good treatment and fair wages that his own father had enjoyed stirred something in his heart; he stood for a moment lost in thought and then said to Mr. Reizman, "I haven't heard or seen a thing. No one came here." Mr. Reizman immediately added my sisters' names to the "list of the living," and thanks to that, Hela and Rivka survived that day.

Here, too, the hand of Divine Providence can be discerned.

It was not mere chance that the *kommissar*'s father had been the manager of Grandfather's soap factory. The merits of our righteous ancestors had stood us in good stead.

At the end of the letter, they asked that we meet them in two days' time, at the same time and place.

Waiting for a train

Where were they taking these people and their children

Chapter Fifteen

My Departure from the Bunker

The next morning, we were once again terrified by heart-rending sobs, cries, and screams. This time, the cries came from the "Metallurgia" factory across the road. Metallurgia was a metal plant, one of the largest in town. My cousin Moshe worked there, together with his wife. When they realized that a selection was imminent, my cousin left his two little children, aged eight and ten, in the hands of one of the Germans, who promised, in exchange for a large sum of money, to keep them safe until the selection was over.

The Germans had finished dragging out the children and adults who had been hiding in Metallurgia, and were already taking them away, when that same German appeared with Moshe's youngsters in hand. On the spot, the Nazis included them in the group bound for the train station, and Treblinka....

The pleading of the distraught parents, their anguished cries, made no impression on these "men of good order." My cousin Moshe survived, as did his wife, but they remained childless and alone. They never had any more children. Moshe's sisters, his brother, and his wife's relatives were all killed by the Germans.

We continued with the routine of our daily life. My father

rationed out equal portions of the carrots and radishes, while David's father warmed water on an electric plate. We agreed that we would drink a cup of hot water twice a day, and that it would be prepared for everyone at once.

After two days, Father and I went out to the garden to "meet" my sisters again. In a soft voice Father called out "Hela!" and immediately we heard Hela and Rivka's response; a shower of vegetables poured through the opening in the wall and, among them, even a few slices of bread wrapped in paper. Happily, I collected this "loot" while Father concentrated on the cherished "dessert" — the letter.

"Tomorrow," wrote my sisters, "they are transferring us and the other workers to a small ghetto, where we will be given a room. That's what they promised." The overnight quarters in the factory were to be liquidated. The workers would come in the morning and go back to the ghetto at night. My sisters thought, said the letter, that Father could send two more girls out just before dawn. "May God grant that all will go well, and you can all get out of the bunker to safety," they concluded.

*   *   *

In the early hours of the next morning, my two sisters and Mrs. Goldman left for the Reizman factory. "Before you leave the factory, send a note so that we may know whether to continue evacuating the bunker," said Father to my sister.

That night, we found a note on the ground. "Carry on!" it said.

Now it was my turn to leave the bunker, together with Chava Goldman. I said goodbye to my beloved parents and little brothers with tears in my eyes and a silent prayer on my lips: "God, help us to pass safely through this path of terror and may I soon see my dear parents and all my family again."

And indeed, God helped me once again. As soon as I arrived, our family friend, Mr. Reizman, with the agreement of the *kommissar*, added my name to the list. That same day I was taken on as a worker, and that evening I went with the others to the Small

Ghetto. There, near the barbed wire gate, sat German and Ukrainian soldiers who carefully counted those entering. For this reason, in order not to increase the numbers of those returning, my sister spent the night at the factory. Later, the Judenrat added my name to the "list of the living" and I became "legal."

Now, we five sisters were all living together in a room on the "family" street. The Small Ghetto consisted of only three streets: one for men, one for women, and one in the middle for couples and families. There was no room for children in this ghetto — it was as if the very idea had been erased from the world.

A high barbed wire fence surrounded the ghetto, and entrance and exit were controlled via the single gate. Night and day, two Ukrainians armed with rifles guarded this gate, and at their side stood a Jewish guard. From shift to shift, Germans from the SS Commando appeared to check that all was as it should be. Close to the ghetto was a German command post, and morning and evening a group of fifteen to twenty Nazis, armed with rifles or submachine guns, would come to show their presence while the outgoing and incoming workers were counted.

In the morning, the workers would gather in the large yard of the old market. Now that I was "legal," I left with my sisters, dressed in a long dress which added — or so I hoped — several years to my insufficient age of thirteen. Group by group, we stood there. A large majority of the workers were sent to the "Hasag" factory where ammunition was manufactured, with others sent to "Rakov," a large plant for processing iron and its derivatives.

Other groups were sent to various worksites, the most important being — for women only — "house cleaning," of Jewish houses of course. I was put in this group of "cleaners."

The houses of the Great Ghetto were already empty of people, and we were instructed to go into the deserted houses and take out — everything. There were silver vessels, valuable crystal objects, dinner services, cutlery, bed linen, etc. Our job was to sort the goods, pack them in parcels, and put them outside the houses.

When everything was outside and tidy, trucks would come and load up the Jewish property. Most of it was sent to Germany. Three girls were sent into each apartment. One would empty the closets, one would pack, and the third would carry the parcels outside.

The Germans supervised the work, patrolling with loaded rifles. In spite of this, some of the girls did manage to take things for themselves — a pair of socks, which they put on right away, a skirt, a blouse.... We had very few clothes, and besides, clothing could be used for trade; even food could be gotten in exchange for clothes.

Any additional morsel was both desired and necessary. The daily bread ration in the ghetto was about 200 grams. A packet of margarine and one-half a pound of sugar had to last an entire week. In addition, every worker got a receipt entitling him to a portion of soup at the general kitchen.

Each working day ended at 6:00 P.M. before dark. We all gathered together at the end of the street and listened to the warning of the German soldier: "Whoever dared to steal from the house in which she worked will be shot." Then we had to organize ourselves in lines, six girls abreast. The Germans would pass among us and look each of us over with murderous eyes. Anyone who looked suspicious would be made to stand in the middle of the road and inspected. If the suspicion proved correct, the soldier would shoot her down in front of us all.

It was a nightmarish scene. One of us would lie there, expiring in her blood, and we were forbidden to extend her any help or succor. Once, a girl tried to go to the help of her friend, and the German, without any hesitation whatsoever, shot her too.

We lived in terror. Therefore no one dared to return a stolen item either. The blows of the rifle butt would reduce the victim to a state not much different from that of the girl who had been shot. This was the routine of our daily life in the Small Ghetto.

Chapter Sixteen

The End of the Bunker

Gradually, we came to the conclusion that it was no longer possible to maintain the bunker, both because of the danger of discovery — which increased each day — and because of the growing difficulty of providing food and water for its occupants. We therefore decided to smuggle the little ones out to the factory in sacks. From there, still stowed away in sacks, they could be smuggled into the ghetto itself.

Mr. Reizman, who wanted to help us, at once agreed to cooperate, and succeeded in influencing the German supervisor to turn a blind eye to Mr. Dziubas and his "relatives"... (he knew nothing of the sacks with the children).

It was decided with Mr. Reizman that the liquidation of the bunker and the absorption of its residents as workers in the factory would take place in two stages, in order to attract the minimum of attention. Since our greatest concern was for the little ones, it was decided that my parents and two little brothers would come first, with David's mother and little sister, while the Kolins, David's father, and David with his brother would leave in the second group. My father promised the Kolins that he would speak to Mr. Reizman and that he would personally come to help them transfer to the factory.

Thus, the first group managed to pass safely to be "absorbed" in the factory, with the little ones stowed in a concealed corner until they could be transferred to the ghetto.

The transfer to the ghetto was more dangerous than getting into the factory, because the Germans, as mentioned, used to count the workers as they went out in the morning and again when they returned at night — and, of course, the numbers had to tally. We were particularly apprehensive of the search that the Germans would conduct upon our return from work that day.

My sisters made an arrangement with a number of workers at the factory that they would spend the night there in order to enable "newcomers" to get into the ghetto. By increasing the number of returnees by one or two per day, it might be possible to "persuade" the guards that some error had occurred in the morning count.

*   *   *

It was a long day, that Tuesday. My sisters and I were again sent to "clean up" houses. After we had arranged ourselves in rows, we were taken back to the Great Ghetto. There, at the cross-roads, the Germans began to divide us up, a few girls to each street. They then allocated us to specific houses. I saw that the Nazi was methodically handing out the work, street by street, one after the other.

"I'll take advantage of this," I said to myself, and waited to be included in the group which would clean the houses on Krutka Street and then managed to get myself included in the trio going into No. 20 — our former home.

I entered the house with mixed feelings. I was glad to have an opportunity to peek into the bunker to see the friends who had remained there. Yet, naturally, my joy was tinged with anxiety. It would not be an easy task to hand over the contents of my own home to the Nazis. I squeezed the two slices of bread which I had put aside for the bunker-stowaways, and hurried off to the bunker.

When I reached the bunker, I stood as though thunder-struck. "Heaven help us! What happened here?" For on the ground, near the well, lay old Mr. Kolin. He had been wounded in the head, and blood streamed down his face. Those well-known and well-liked features... I had parted from them not so very long ago! It seemed that he had only recently been shot.

Shocked and frightened, I could not touch him or even approach him. Frozen in place like a pillar of salt, I stood by the well, unable to tear my eyes away. "Maybe he'll recognize me," I thought to myself. "Maybe he'll give me some signal." But he did not move. After a few minutes, I pulled myself together and forced myself to look beyond this gruesome scene, towards the bunker itself. The door was open and everything was shattered. I drew closer and gave a feeble cry, hoping that someone there would hear my voice.

Silence!!!

Faintness overcame me and I felt that I would soon lose control and pass out. I stood for a while without moving, my mind was a vacuum, devoid of all thought. Slowly, slowly, I gathered strength and forced myself back to consciousness. It was not easy. What had happened to my beloved parents? Where were my brothers? Had they managed to get out of the bunker before it was exposed? What about the others? These torturous questions swarmed in my brain unanswered. Suddenly, I noticed that I was still holding my hand to my side. Why? I asked myself. Then I recalled the slices of bread. I had fasted for almost two days to save them — it never occurred to me that I would have to keep them....

My instinct for survival interrupted my reverie and whispered: "More than half an hour has passed. The Germans will soon come to see the progress of the work." I began to run towards our apartment and made straight for the linen cupboard. First, I took out the Czech tablecloths which Father brought home for Mother from his business trips to Carlsbad and Marienbad. All the tablecloths were arranged according to size, beautifully wrapped and tied with orange ribbon. Next came the hand-embroidered bed linen, magnificently arranged, precisely folded by Mother's loving hand. Every shelf was decorated with Swiss lace... how much love and affection Mother had lavished on that closet!

"I mustn't think of that," I told myself. The creak of heavy boots could already be heard outside, and I hurried to place two of the packed parcels outside the door.

"Sorry for the delay," I told my workmates. "I'll show you where the good dinner services are kept... don't forget to pack them all!"

At last, we heard the siren: the signal to stop work. It was 6:00 P.M. We presented ourselves for the roll call in rows of six girls, and were then taken the distance to the ghetto with Germans on each side of us, loaded rifles in their hands.

Exhausted and brokenhearted, I returned home. My heart was filled with deep sorrow, and I could not halt the whirlwind of my thoughts: What had befallen my parents? Where were my little brothers? What had happened to Mrs. Kolin, to David's parents, to David, and to his sisters? How had the bunker been disclosed?

My sisters were busy with preparations for the eagerly anticipated happy reunion and did not pay any attention to me. They did not know that I had "cleaned" our own house that day. I withdrew and sat in a corner, unable to eat. I felt that I couldn't swallow even a single drop of water.

I sat and listened to my excited sisters: "Another hour and we'll see them all! Even less!" they said to each other. They talked longingly, as if my parents were returning from a distant land and not from only a few hundred meters away. Happily they filled a bucket of water and even placed a basin, slightly cracked, for the ritual hand-washing. "How nice this room is compared to the bunker," I thought, "even if the walls are dirty, and there's mildew in the corners...." At that moment the mildew stains seemed to my eyes like works of art decorating the walls.

Chapter Seventeen

Waiting for Our Parents

Tense with excitement, we waited for Father, Mother, Chanoch, and Yisroelik. According to the plan, the children were to leave the bunker hidden in sacks. David's mother and his little sister would also come along.

We five sisters who were now in the ghetto scrubbed the room which we had been given on the street reserved for families, and tried as much as possible, under the existing conditions, to give it the look of home. We obtained some beds, and near a rickety table we lovingly set a few chairs, each one different from the next. We also found a little closet, admittedly missing one leg, which we fixed up with an "artificial limb" made out of a box which almost exactly matched the space left by the missing part.

"It's 7:30, let's go," announced my oldest sister happily. I went out with the others to the ghetto gate. I did not, however, share my sisters' joy; my own heart was full of sadness. Again and again I saw before my eyes Mr. Kolin, lying wounded and bloodied on the ground, and the bunker, breached and exposed. I prayed silently to God in Heaven not to disappoint us all: "Please, please, let us see our family, whole and united again...."

I stood and waited as if my insides were hollow; it was 8:00 P.M., then 8:30. Everyone had already returned from all the various work places. At 9:00, the Germans left and two Ukrainians and a Jewish policeman remained. The gate groaned shut and was locked, and the guards disappeared inside the command post. Silence descended upon the ghetto. My sisters looked at each other and said, "It doesn't look as if they'll come today."

"But we haven't seen Reizman's workers!"

"Maybe they got back before 7:30?"

"Let's wait a little longer. No one has driven us away yet."

We waited. Night had long since fallen and wrapped us all in a dark veil. We were tense, but still did not relinquish hope. Then we heard footsteps in the distance. "Someone is coming!" said my sister.

"Who can it be so late?" We strained our eyes. The steps drew nearer and sounded louder.

"It's Reizman's workers!" announced my oldest sister.

My heart took courage once more. Would our parents be among them? When the people were within a few meters of the gate, the Ukrainians reluctantly came out of their warm huts and hurled insults at the returning workers, especially at the Jew responsible for them.

"If you come late again," shouted the Ukrainians, "you'll stay out all night! Quick, Quick!"

They pushed everyone inside with yells and shouts and slammed the gates behind them. Quickly, they locked all the locks and hurried back into their warm houses.

And then, the most miraculous thing: my parents, and David's mother, too, were in the group — all with sacks in their hands.

The Ukrainians, annoyed by the late return of the workers, did not bother to check them at all, and thus they were able to bring the sacks — and the children inside them — into the ghetto.

My sisters took the sacks from my parents and went into the first courtyard in the ghetto, to set the little "prisoners" free.

Chanoch, Yisroelik, and David's little sister were truly happy to feel the solid ground under their feet. They had been confined in the sacks for so long, frozen in fear, with hardly any air to breathe.

The little ones knew only too well what their fate would have been had they been discovered.

Now, the whole family marched towards our new home.

"We were so worried," said my sisters. "We waited and waited...."

"It's my fault," said Father. "I asked the factory workers for a special favor. I was informed that the guards usually carry out a search on every package brought into the ghetto, and I was afraid for the fate of our precious 'parcels.' I thought that by being so very late, and with the help of our Almighty Father, we might manage to successfully smuggle them in."

"Thank God." I hugged Chanoch, and though my hands still trembled, my heart overflowed with joy.

We all crowded into the one room, together with David's mother and sister. We honored Father and Mother with two beds, and all the rest of us managed with the two remaining ones. But we were together, a roof over our heads, hot food in our stomachs, and so, I felt, we could overcome all the sorrows in the world, as long as my parents — so dear to my heart, inseparable from us like an atom which cannot be split — as long as they were with us.

That night I awoke many times, haunted by the memory of Mr. Kolin. Was he perhaps still alive? Had he needed help? From time to time, I touched my mother and drew comfort from her presence. This was no dream, Mother was there near me. And silently I thanked the Almighty that we had been granted this great privilege of being reunited.

The next day, my brother-in-law also returned to the ghetto, alive and well. He had been working elsewhere for the past seven weeks.

*   *   *

We had now been in the ghetto for two weeks. It was two

We were all together in a room in the Small Ghetto, and so, I felt, we could overcome all the sorrows in the world.

months since the deportation of the Jews of Czenstochow. Our daily routine continued. We still worked at "cleaning" Jewish homes, and we now had a strong motive to "pinch" things at every opportunity. I always tried to wear something back, be it a skirt, a shirt, or socks. Sometimes, despite the cold, I went to work without a coat in order to bring things back for my family. I would even place sheets or pillowcases about my person. I allowed myself to do this despite the repeated warnings of the Germans, not only because I was thin and the added "weight" did not show on me, but also because I felt it was my duty. My aim was to ease things for my dear parents and family. My parents were in a difficult situation because they were "illegal," and thus anything I brought for use or sale was helpful. The single closet in our room was completely empty — we couldn't even change our one towel.

One day, it fell to my lot to "clean" on Nadrzeczna Street, where my friend Marilka had lived. With beating heart I entered the apartment. "Where are Marilka's parents?" I could not help wondering. "Marilka herself, where is she?"

I opened Marilka's clothes closet: the garments hung tidily and peacefully, as if Marilka had only gone away on a holiday. Without much hesitation, I slipped on her summer coat; she had apparently taken her winter one when she left the house. We were of similar build, and the coat fitted as if made to measure. I would return it to her. Or perhaps Father would pay Marilka's mother for the coat and she would buy another.... I promised myself again that I would take care of Marilka's coat.

That day, I returned to the ghetto depressed. I thought of the forty children in my class — not one of them remained. Our *komplet* of fifteen girls — where were they, all of them? Where had the Germans sent them?

Probably they were worse off than we were. Here in the ghetto, among Jews, I felt more secure and tranquil. We were brothers, sharing a common fate, and we knew our suffering was

solely because of our Jewishness. We shared a feeling of brother-
hood, that "All Israel is responsible for one another." Also, there
was plenty of water, and although food was scarce, it was provided regularly. Certainly an improvement over the bunker,
where we could not tell dark from light, nor Shabbat from the
weekdays.

The word Shabbat warmed my heart, especially now in the
ghetto. On Friday, Mother would prepare several dishes for Shabbat, and in the evening we would spread the table with a white
sheet and Mother would stick two candles in a baked potato and
recite the blessing over them. On Thursday night, we all managed to wash in honor of Shabbat using a sliver of soap I had
smuggled in. I knew I was endangering myself by bringing it, but
in view of the satisfaction it would bring to my whole family, it
was worth it to me.

I will never forget that Shabbat night in the ghetto, the first
after we had all left the bunker. My whole being was filled with
gratitude to the Almighty for my parents — and for Shabbat. To
me, these were the most wonderful things in the world. I felt so
good that I wished this beautiful night would never end. I fought
sleep, although I knew I had to get up early for roll call and work.
Tiredness overcame me, and I felt my eyes closing. A sweet smile
lit up my face — a smile of bliss and contentment. I fell asleep.

Selection to left side ("to death")

Chapter Eighteen

Rumors from Treblinka

Some days later, the workers at the Reizman factory told us what had happened in the bunker near our home. It seems that those in hiding had spoken loudly among themselves — perhaps an argument had broken out. Their voices had been heard by a passing German. The bunker was broken into. Mr. Kolin was shot on the spot, and the others — David, his father, and Mrs. Kolin were sent to Treblinka....

At this time, strange and varied bits of news and information began to filter through to us regarding the fate of the deportees. Two men returned from the death camps and told us what was being done there. People refused to believe them. "Those two have, apparently, gone crazy," they said to each other. "How could it be that in the twentieth century people are being destroyed by poison gas. That men, women, and children are being indiscriminately killed?

Nevertheless, the anxiety in our hearts grew and deepened; the stories sounded depraved, but those who told them were not insane. One of the returnees who had escaped from the death camp at Treblinka told us that he had, by a miracle, managed to crawl under a train and cling to its underside until it reached Czenstochow. "All the way, the noise of the wheels pounded in my brain with a monotonous rhythm, like the Chinese water torture, and all that way I clung to a single goal — to tell all. To tell what is really going on. Perhaps some Jewish lives can be saved if they know what it is they face. For this reason I felt that my suffering was worthwhile." He gazed at the faces around him, faces frozen in terror.

"Don't worry. The world-renowned German organization and order doesn't let you down. Human beings are led to the gas chambers with no notion of where they are being taken, and the line doesn't even falter. Their last steps are made more pleasant by musical accompaniment. Men and women are separated. "Go to have a wash before you go into the camp," say the orders. Each one carries a sliver of soap, but as soon as they enter the "showers" they are engulfed in Cyclon-B, a poison gas, instead of water.... The bodies are then removed from the other side of the gas chamber.

"Within only a few hours," he added in a hoarse voice, "the hair of young men turned grey because of what they had witnessed... I saw it with my own eyes."

It's no wonder that we found it hard to accept and believe this reality, if even eyewitnesses to these atrocities found it hard to absorb. One of the escapees said that he had seen his own family among the heaps of dead bodies. "I thought I was dreaming, having a nightmare. I rubbed my eyes and pinched myself — no, this was no dream...."

The older people just couldn't accept these horrible stories, but the younger ones began to think, to hint, to devise plans.

*   *   *

This was in December, 1942. An icy frost fell and there was nothing with which to heat the room — but as long as we were together, and could gather each evening to exchange news of the day's events, we were warm. I thanked God that we were not in the bunker but in a room, where we could speak freely and where, when it was cold, one could hop from one leg to the other. We could even have a hot drink at night, and there was plenty of water. I wished that we could stay like that for the duration of the war. However, in a corner of our hearts a feeling of fear for our brother, Mendel, nagged. For despite his promise, he had not returned to us. I knew he had been sent to Treblinka, but I still hoped that he had managed to escape. He was surely hiding somewhere and would someday return.... I firmly quieted my anxiety. With God's help, all would be well.

In the meantime, petty trade continued apace in the ghetto. The factory workers would bring food which they bought from the Poles, and we "cleaning" workers would bring clothes or bedding which they, in turn, would "buy" from us — and then again sold to the Poles for food, and so on. Business was conducted on our street, "the families" street. We did not engage in trade for its own sake, but rather, because it was the only way that we could acquire the basic necessities of life. From seven in the evening onwards people would bring out chairs or benches, and on these they would place their wares. Our side of the street was the clothes market, while across the street they sold food. Trade continued until 10:00 P.M., when the lights were turned off and the use of electricity was forbidden.

At that hour, by order of the Nazis, three Jewish musicians would play a funeral march by Brahms. At dawn, these same musicians would strike up lively and cheerful music to arouse us for work.

Officially, this was a work camp for young people. Children were unmentionable. But within a month, the tension lessened somewhat and the small children who had been smuggled into the ghetto from the various hideouts began to peep out. The Judenrat decided to open a kindergarten for them, and the Germans gave their "agreement." Some Jews got hold of a few toys and some dolls, and a young girl, a kindergarten teacher by profession, cared for the children and kept them occupied throughout the day. There were only thirty-five to forty children in the whole ghetto.

Father also sent Yisroelik, aged six, to the nursery, albeit unwillingly. "If the Germans know about the nursery, it is no good," he maintained. But his friends and acquaintances persuaded him. "A boy of six who spends all of his time with adults will not develop well." Besides, the alternative was to keep him hidden as he had been until now, all day long, under a bed together with his brother, Chanoch, so that they scarcely saw the light of day. In the end, Father gave in and Yisroelik went to the kindergarten.

One day, a Wednesday, I stayed home with my little brothers. It often happened that when I reported for work, I was told that I was too young. On such occasions, I stayed home and hid with the boys. At 9:30 in the morning, Yisroelik came running home, terrified and excited, his head bare. "Don't be angry," he panted, "I ran and my hat fell off. Germans with guns came to the kindergarten and put all the children on a truck."

"Almighty God! All the children?"

"Some children managed to escape. Me, too. I didn't want to pick up my hat; I was afraid those awful Nazis would put me on the truck, too."

"You're a smart boy," I kissed him with relief.

"I'm telling you," the child could not calm down, "the streets are full of Nazis. I think they're looking for more children."

I seized his thin little hand and that of Chanoch and ran to our sister Hela's room. Like other married couples, my older sister and her husband had been given a room of their own, which was close to ours. There, Father, ever-anxious since Yisroelik had started going to the kindergarten, had built a sort of mini-bunker for the children to hide in. There was a niche in the wall about twenty-five centimeters wide, and in front of this he placed a cupboard. He took one of the boards out of the back of the cupboard and fixed it so that it could be removed and replaced in case of need, and this served as the door of the niche. Carefully, I took out the board, put Yisroelik — and after him Chanoch — inside, and then squeezed myself in, slipping the board back into place. For eight long hours we stayed there in absolute silence, and not a sound escaped our lips.

Chapter Nineteen

Liquidation of the Kindergarten

S chneller!" the guttural shouts of the Germans could be heard outside. "*Raus!*" (Quicker! Out!)

Heartrending wails of adults and children followed in the wake of the shouts. We trembled and pressed back against the wall of our bunker in Hela's room, as if the wall could serve as our shield.

The barks of the dogs which accompanied the "masters" froze our blood. Voices drew nearer, and suddenly, they were in the room there with us... we were as still as pillars of salt; we were afraid even to breathe. I was terrified of the dogs. I knew that if they were given the order to find human beings, we were lost, for they were trained to do just that, to discover hideouts and bunkers and to sniff out people.

Our three hearts beat with a single rhythm. From time to time, I stroked Yisroelik's little head to soothe him, my hand trembling with fear. In turn, his and Chanoch's presence gave me support and encouragement. In total darkness, with scarcely any air, we stayed thus for hours. We lost all sense of time. But we knew that when everyone returned to the ghetto we would hear their voices, and then we could come out.

At night, we heard Hela searching for us and came out of our hiding place. It was a joyful surprise for our anxious and worried parents. Neighbors had told them that they heard from the workers in the public soup kitchen that all of the children from the kindergarten had been taken on the back of a truck to an unknown destination. According to general consensus only three or four children had managed to escape, and my parents did not dare to hope that our Yisroelik might be among them.

The fact that the Germans had suddenly come in the early hours of the morning had added to their anxiety — perhaps I had not realized, and thus had not managed to hide myself and the children in time.

How happy we were that we were once again reunited with our family in our "home."

*   *   *

In this selection the Germans had taken 800 people, who were collected within a few hours and sent by train together with Jews from another town — to Treblinka. The Jewish population of Czenstochow was 30,000 at the outbreak of World War II. Immediately at the beginning of the war, large numbers of people came there from the neighboring villages and towns, doubling the population in the space of only a few months. When the Ghetto in Lodz was already in operation, our situation was still comparatively good, and Jewish refugees continued to arrive. After the *aktion* only about 5,000 Jews remained in Czenstochow legally, while in actuality the number was about twice that, above 10,000. The Jews hid in the ghetto and outside, in hideouts and bunkers, and after some weeks reached the Small Ghetto.

Here too, the Jews, and we ourselves among them, did not find peace. We had barely breathed a sigh of relief at the end of the last selection, and immediately there was another one. This time, too, I had remained at home because the Jew in charge of the workplace had said to me: "Girl, please find yourself another victim!"

"What do you mean?"

"I mean, please give your place to a more efficient worker."

Thus, my long dresses had once again failed, accompanied as they were by my "advanced" age, thirteen and a half years. This was not the first time that I had been sent away from a job, but this time the foreman hadn't even bothered to apologize! Until now, they had always explained that they were afraid of the Germans. This time, even the pain of rejection was not spared me.

That same day, Yisroelik had gone out to play outside the house. The neighborhood was full of junk which had been thrown out of the houses when people moved in. At 10:00 A.M. the child came home, pale and frightened. "I heard voices...Germans are coming... searches... selections...."

I didn't wait for further explanation, but seized both my brothers and climbed with them to the attic above our room. We lay there on the floor, because there was no room to stand or even to sit. No sooner were we lying down than we already heard the familiar hated sounds: German shouts, barking dogs, and, after them, the shocked, wailing voices of mothers and children.

We heard them enter the room and, with the help of the Jewish police, search beneath the beds, where Chanoch used to hide, and inside the closet. We held our breath, but our hearts beat like sledgehammers. I was afraid that their pounding would give us away, and I clenched my teeth. My body was bathed in cold sweat; one more minute, one more heartbeat, and we would be exposed...."Please, Merciful and Forgiving One, don't let us fall prey to these wolves...."

My prayer was heard. After a thorough search the Germans left, and with them, those terrible predatory dogs.

We did not hasten to leave, but stayed a long time afterwards in the attic without moving. I felt as if my hands and feet had become detached from me and would no longer obey me.... But slowly the German voices faded and sounded only occasionally, each time from further and further away. Later on, when we heard the voices of our family, we lowered the shaky ladder we had pulled up into the attic with us, and came down again.

*   *   *

One night, several days after that day of terror, I went over to Yisroelik, who lay sleepless on his bed, and sat down beside him.

"It's so late, Yisroelik, why aren't you asleep?"

"Tell me, Rutka," was his surprising response, "can you die just because you want to?"

"Die? Because you want to? However did you get such an idea?"

"I think," said the little one innocently, "that when they put us on trains and send us to Treblinka, I will look out through the opening in the wagon at the forests, fields, and flowers, and when we get the order *"Raus!"* ("Out!") to go out to the gas chambers, I want to close my eyes and die.... Do you think you can order death?'

My eyes filled with tears, but I swallowed them and kissed his eyelids.

"You will live, Yisroelik, and grow big, and you'll come safely through this awful war with us...don't think such thoughts."

I tucked his blankets around him and returned to my own bed. I looked anxiously at my mother. Had she heard our conversation? Thank God, she hadn't. No one else had heard us.

That night, I tossed and turned for a long time on my bed. The weight on my heart would not let me sleep.

Where had little Yisroelik heard these stories? It seemed that while he pretended to play, he had all the while listened in on the grown-ups' conversations about the atrocities at Auschwitz and Treblinka. The little children took it all in silently and knew exactly how serious our situation was.

Where were they taking these people and their children?

Chapter Twenty

The Great Selection

On January 3, 1943, a large group of Nazis returned to "visit" the ghetto. This time they came in the late afternoon. All those found in the ghetto were sent to the old marketplace outside the gate of the ghetto for a roll call. A loudspeaker transmitted this order through the three streets of the ghetto, with the additional warning that anyone found in the ghetto during the search that would take place following the roll call would be shot.

At the time, I was working on Third Street, where a large clothing warehouse had been set up in a spacious hall. Great piles of clothing were spread out along its length: dresses, blouses, skirts, and trousers. Every few days, trucks would pull up in front of the warehouse and unload a delivery of men's, women's, and children's clothing. These garments were then sorted by the Jewish workers who were responsible for the warehouse. New clothes were piled along the left of the hall and used ones on the opposite side.

All garments were examined for foreign currency or gold, which was sometimes found sewn into the cloth or concealed in special buttons. It sometimes happened that one of the Jewish workers managed to take some valuable object for himself, and therefore the Germans supervised the work very closely.

When the order to assemble for roll call was announced, all

the workers, including those of the ghetto kitchen and bakery, were required to attend. I, however, made up my mind not to go. I was well aware that although I was already thirteen and a half years old, and considered myself quite grown-up, in the eyes of most people I was only a little girl. I also knew that I could not make it back to our home in time to hide my brothers; it was too late. I figured that my parents had already returned from work, and they would manage to hide them. Father and Mother were now registered with the Judenrat, and their residence in the ghetto was therefore "legal."

It was nearly 6:00 P.M. No living soul remained in the warehouse, all the workers had already left. Suddenly, an idea struck me — I would hide here, in the piles of clothing! No sooner said than done. I dived into a thick pile of heaped-up bed linens. I left myself only one concealed peephole and a small opening for one ear, where I could listen to what was happening.

The screams started a quarter of an hour later. I knew that this meant that the searches had started. I burrowed deeper into my pile. Through the layers of bed linens, the shouts of the Germans could be clearly heard. Suddenly, I sensed that someone was standing beside my heap and toying with its contents. He kept lifting off several layers of sheets with the tip of his stick. I did not dare burrow further into the pile, for fear that the Germans would spot the movement.

He carried on with his game, and each time more linens were lifted off. One more...and another one. Oh God, this was the end...any minute now, I would be exposed...and then the German would pull out his gun and shoot me as one does a mad dog.... My strength failed me.

I don't know how long the game went on. To me, it seemed like ages. In my heart, I asked God not to give me over to these murderers: "Please God, help me!"

Then I heard the German say, "I don't think there's any point searching here. They're all at the market."

After a long, long time, when I dared to move a little, I noticed that my face had been covered by only a single pillow case.

I began to stretch my cramped arms and legs and to recover somewhat. I thanked our Father in Heaven for his great mercy and kindness, for not abandoning me at this crucial moment. "Lord of the Universe, please let me be saved with all of my dear family and the whole Jewish people...."

Little by little, I rose and listened. Outside, silence reigned. An ominous silence. Thoughts raced through my head: Where were my parents? Had they gone back to the ghetto? Where were my little brothers? Had they managed to hide? And my sisters? Were they still at the marketplace?

I decided to wait in a corner of the warehouse until I heard Jewish voices. I realized that another selection had taken place and that people had been sent to Treblinka. But where, I wondered, were the others? The Germans always sent only part of the people. Why did the others not return? For a long time, I crouched in that dark corner, between the mounds of clothing.

"Whose clothes are these?" The question crossed my mind, "From where do the Germans bring them?" My heart shrank.

It was over an hour later that I heard the hushed whispers and faint weeping of our brethren returning to the ghetto. Then I came out of my corner and ran home.

The whole family was gathered in our room and greatly worried for my safety. Then I noticed — Father was missing! I looked at my darling mother and saw tears in her eyes — my sisters, my brothers, everyone was crying.

Where was my dearest, beloved father? Why had he not returned? I couldn't contain myself, but burst into bitter tears. My sister Rivka rose from her place and came over to me.

"I'll tell you what happened," she said. "A friend of Father's told me; he was beside him all the while...."

She stopped, swallowed, breathed deeply, and continued:

"Everyone gathered in the market and the Germans carried

out a huge selection. Several hundred young people were taken off, supposedly for work, and were sent to the train station to be loaded into boxcars, taking them off...somewhere.

"When the *aktion* ended, one of the Germans asked: 'We need twenty men to work for a few hours. Who will volunteer?'

"Father got up and joined the group of volunteers. The German looked him over and said: 'You, Jew, you're too old to work,' and with a wave of his hand sent him to the right, to the line of people who had been selected to go to Treblinka.

"All those people were sent to Radomsk," concluded Rivka. In Radomsk, a large Polish city, a train waited, already filled with people who had been "selected" there. The long train then took them all off to an unknown destination.

I found out afterwards that my mother immediately asked our cousin, Micha Birenzweig, to help. He was clever, enterprising, and "popular" with some of the Germans. He was a sort of entrepreneur and, as such, useful to them. Micha, who was married to our cousin Hania Scheinfeld, right away asked his superiors, three SS men, to take Father off the deportation contingent. They, however, answered that he could not be found. The carriages had already been added to the Radomsk train and locating him would have been like looking for a needle in a haystack.

I looked again at my mother, my sisters, my brothers — they were all sad and downcast, and tears streamed from their eyes. I too joined in the silent "chorus."

Chapter Twenty-one

The Doctors Entrapped

The clock showed 1:00 A.M. and tomorrow we would have to get up at 5:00 A.M., as usual, for roll call. It was high time for us to get some sleep. Yisroelik and Chanoch got into Father's bed and cried silently. I, and certainly the others, too, did not get a wink of sleep. In the morning we all got up with red, swollen eyes.

For a long time I continued to believe that my father was still alive. I just could not accept any other possibility. Even after the war, I still clung to the hope that one day he would return from "somewhere".... Perhaps he had escaped to Siberia, perhaps he had joined the partisans in the forests. After all, anything was possible.

The great *aktion* had indeed broken up many families, and a lot of people had remained alone, although somehow there was always a brother, sister, or cousin who could make up the remnants of a "family." This selection had hit almost every family. The tension increased, and no one could be sure if he would live out the day. Even Micha Birenzweig, our sharp and lively cousin — who, in the goodness of his heart, had more than once helped to ease our lot — even he did not manage to escape.

Micha's status was such that he was allowed to work alongside an Aryan, even without a distinguishing "Jewish" armband. He even traveled outside the town. This continued until the Ger-

The people worked in the bitter and penetrating cold.

mans in charge of him began to feel that Micha knew too many of their secrets and decided to eliminate him. One morning, several Nazis arrived at his place of work with the intention of permanently silencing him. Micha noticed that his "bosses" had come with some other murderers; he said farewell to my mother, who worked in the same *mebelager* (furniture warehouse), and beat a hasty retreat. The Germans hunted him with tracker dogs but, to their great chagrin, did not find him.

Several weeks passed. There was no trace of Micha, and he was almost forgotten. Then, disaster struck: a certain gentile was missing from work for several days, and the Germans went to his house outside the town in order to force him to come back to work. There, in the gentile's apartment, they recognized Micha and shot him on the spot. This story was told to me by a Polish woman who later worked with me in the Rakov factory.

*   *   *

Winter was now at its height, and the cold was bitter and penetrating. I worked with my sister Rivka clearing the railway tracks of snow. I worked with a blunt, heavy tool, and it was hard work. I was still a young girl, and not very strong physically, and some of the Poles would take pity on me and invite me to warm myself at their stoves. Rivka also kept an eye on me and always tried to work nearby to help me with any difficulties I encountered.

We were made to walk to our workplace in lines of six women, while armed Germans guarded us on both sides. In order to entertain themselves, they ordered us to sing, teaching us German marching songs which we chanted both going to work and returning, exhausted, at night. Sometimes, as we went through the Christian neighborhoods, gentiles would come out of their houses, lean on their gates, and call out to us: "Still alive Jews? And so many of you!" Our hearts shrank at the sight of "Yanek" or "Antek," who scarcely knew how to sign their names, gorging themselves on good food and gloating over the Jewish property they had acquired, while we starved. They were now the "masters." This is not to say that all the Poles behaved in this way, but the majority of them certainly did.

We would continue on our way, reaching the streets of the Great Ghetto. The doors and windows of the houses hung open, and death peeped out from them. Where are you, I would think, you men, women, and children who had lived there? The uncles, aunts, dozens of cousins, the boys and girls who had filled our streets? Where had they vanished, the old men and women whose dignity had graced their surroundings and given meaning to our young lives? And where, too, were the *talmidei chachamim*, the scholars, whose sharp discourses and discussions had added spice to our lives, dispensing to us youngsters their words of wisdom, laced with an abundance of Jewish humor? All had vanished, leaving behind an unbearable desolation.

Sunk in thoughts such as these, I would suddenly shake myself to find the German sentry glaring at me. With an aching heart I would burst into German song. If only he would just leave me in peace. Thoughts, in spite of everything, were private property, and I could still think without having to report....

On this particular day, we reached the railway tracks and cleaned them of their burden of snow and ice. Suddenly we heard a clanking and rattling, and a long train of about thirty freight cars and two third-class coaches pulled in. Many Jewish doctors and their families were traveling in the third-class carriages.

The people on the train tried to communicate with us in Polish and Yiddish and asked us questions. Conversation with them was forbidden to us, but we tried to get closer and warn them what lay ahead of them. This was in February 1943, and our information was more up-to-date than theirs. "We're from Bialystock," they told us. "The Germans are taking us to work camps."

"Work camps? They are death camps! Don't believe what they tell you!"

"No, it can't be so. The Germans have allowed us to take our medical instruments and even some of our property.... You're mistaken!"

We did manage to convince one doctor, who stepped down from his third-class carriage and mingled with us. One of the men quickly gave the newcomer his armband so that he wouldn't be noticed.

As for the doctors of Czenstochow, the "special relationship" towards them continued. A few days later, it was announced that the doctors of the Small Ghetto were to present

View of the Small Ghetto

themselves, with their families, in the old marketplace. A rumor
immediately began to circulate that they were being sent to Eretz
Yisrael. The Germans then announced over the loudspeaker that
several dozen entry permits to Palestine had been received for
doctors and their families. There were those among us who
sensed a trap, others who tended to believe. In any case, at the
appointed hour the doctors went to the old marketplace, dressed

in their best clothes, hats on their heads, as befitted members of the medical profession about to travel abroad.

We stood behind the barbed wire fence that enclosed the ghetto and watched them with envy. Behind us was an elderly doctor, all alone, whose family had been sent to Treblinka in the first *aktion*. He could not manage to push his way through the masses of people who had gathered near the barbed wire fence. He stood pleading with them to let him get to the marketplace. However, the Jews stood as if hypnotized, gazing at the "chosen" outside, and did not heed his pleas. Thus, the elderly doctor was not able to go out, to Eretz Yisrael....

To his good fortune and ours, he remained in the ghetto, the only Jewish doctor besides the refugee from Bialystock.

The others, with their families, were taken by truck to the cemetery in Czenstochow. There the Germans ordered the doctors to dig "trenches" and when they had done so, made them line up on the edge. The Germans then shot the children, the women, and, finally, the doctors themselves.

We were told this by Poles who lived near the cemetery and who were eyewitnesses to the massacre, which took place on Shabbat, the eve of Purim, March 20, 1943.

After selection they are taking to death...

Chapter Twenty-two

Jaundice

W hat's wrong Rutka?"

"I don't feel well...a bit weak. I'll get over it."

As if to deny this optimistic declaration, a knife-sharp pain passed through my stomach.

"Oh, no," I thought in panic, "it's forbidden to be ill in the ghetto!"

Even so, I could not dispel the dreadful stomach pains and diarrhea which left me very weak.

I dreaded a prolonged stay in the ghetto's little hospital. I knew that anyone remaining there for longer than a week was sent "away."

The SS officer, Dagenhart, who was in charge of the ghetto, would visit the hospital regularly, and woe to the person who he saw there twice. He never failed to interrogate the doctors regarding the duration of their patients' stay, the nature of their illnesses, and even ascertained their names. Knowing this, I staggered home and went to bed. My mother was filled with consternation by my condition.

"Call a doctor," she told my sister in a low voice, while putting a thermometer in my mouth. "Take your temperature," she told me. It was very high.

The old doctor who had been left behind in the ghetto arrived within the hour. He took one look at me and confirmed:

"Jaundice! She must go to the hospital."

"The hospital!" said my mother anxiously. "Why can't I nurse her here at home?"

"No, don't do that," said the doctor. "The medical care at the hospital is very good."

"But..." my mother tried to argue.

"Understand," interrupted the doctor, "you are endangering both yourself and your daughter. If you leave her in the ghetto, the two of you are likely to be caught in one of the searches, and then...."

There was no need to continue. My mother relented. My sisters sat me on a chair and carried me between them to the next street. From time to time they stopped to gather strength and change sides, blessing the concealing veil of darkness.

Twenty minutes later we reached our destination. A nurse took me from them and sent them home.

"We'll come back tomorrow, Rutka," they promised, seeing my glum face. "We'll come and visit you the minute we finish work!"

Conditions in the hospital were very poor. It was located in an old, run-down apartment. The beds were set out in rows, each one boasting a different color and appearance. The room looked like a secondhand furniture store. The walls were not outstanding in their cleanliness, but it was heated — a great point in its favor! With the last remnants of my strength, I crawled into bed and curled up beneath the blanket. All I wanted to do was to rest. I fell asleep.

I was awakened the next morning by a tiny ray of sunshine peeping in on me. How happy I was to see it. Through the window I could see only a grey wall, but I imagined that there was a tree growing nearby, with green leaves and a bird's nest hidden in its boughs. I was even sure that I could hear the sound of happy chirping....

I thanked God that I was in a warm apartment, getting

medical care. I only asked to be speedily restored to health and to the bosom of my family. In spite of the hard conditions "at home," I didn't complain. I wanted to be together with the others, to feel and see my mother, sisters, and brothers whom I loved more than anything in the world.

That day, towards nightfall, my mother and sisters visited me. They even brought me a piece of cake, but I was unable to eat it and sent it back for my two little brothers.

To my good fortune, my condition improved rapidly, and after a week or so my mother took me home again. The day after I left, there was a selection and several girls were sent "away."

I stayed home alone for several days, since I was still very weak and unfit for work. My little brothers took care of me — and of our house. Every half-hour they would come to my bed and report on what was happening outside. Only after 6:00 P.M. did they dare sit by my bed, and then I would tell them lovely stories from the recent past. I wanted to take them out of the sad present, even if only for a little while, and to transport them to another world, more joyful and happy. To my delight, I saw that they followed my stories closely and asked all kinds of questions.

Although our home was cold, I could already feel the first stirrings of spring. Through the window I could see a scrap of blue sky and the happy smile of sunshine. My heart pounded with joy. How I thanked our Father in heaven that I had recovered from my serious illness! My heart was once more filled with hope for a new tomorrow which would be, with God's help, better.

Chapter Twenty-three

Last Greetings from Marilka

I n spite of everything, daily life had to go on, including the petty trading and smuggling. Sometimes I would ask one of the Polish women to buy food for me in exchange for money. When she brought the bread, cheese, or milk, I would hide them in my jacket before going back to the ghetto. The Germans conducted thorough searches of our tools several times a week, near the gate of the ghetto. When this check (it was called *"revisia"*) started, it was obvious that everyone would be searched and a whispered warning would quickly pass from one row to the next: *"Revisia!"*

The members of the group would quickly distribute their "property"; in this way, at least others would eat their fill. The food passed from hand to hand and included all kinds of good things: sausage, bread, salted and smoked fish, butter, and cheese of various sorts. There was drink, too, beer and milk.

Every checkup caused heavy losses, and that evening and the next day the prices of goods would rise so much that even bread or stale cakes would be outrageously expensive. Even so, the Jews went on "importing" and continued to take risks. Some were successful in their dealings and even "made it rich."

My two older sisters were now working in the Hasag ammunition factory, which operated round-the-clock, seven days a week. Rivka and I were sent to work at the Rakov factory, which

extracted lead-iron from soil. Different kinds of tools and implements were produced from this iron, such as iron filaments
(wires), rods, and spare pans, by casting liquid iron into various
molds as required. My mother continued to work in the furniture
warehouse, and the two little ones, Chanoch and Yisroelik,
stayed home. The door was always left open, and they took turns
keeping watch, listening for the slightest sound of activity outside. They both developed a strong sense of caution and extremely acute hearing.

Sometimes, on quiet days, when the Germans did not come
into the ghetto, the little ones allowed themselves a stroll near
the kitchen. One of my sisters worked there, and when she saw
them outside she would bring them her soup or her bread ration.
She would not get another one that day but would make do with
whatever she could scrape out of the dirty pots she washed. Nevertheless, she would often give up her ration, so that my little
brothers, who were still "illegal," would have what to eat. The
Germans could reduce us to poverty, beat us, kill us, but they
could not take from us that nobility of spirit that was our Jewish
heritage.

The young people of the ghetto began to whisper of revolt.
It was said that there were plans underway. There were also rumors that we possessed arms — a few rifles and homemade Molo-
tov cocktails. There was a difference of opinion between the
younger people and the older folk. The latter declared that rebel-
lion would bring disaster and would end in the total liquidation
of the ghetto. They claimed that there was a chance the war
would end and that the ghetto would be saved. Some of the
young people, on the other hand, maintained that if we just sat
and waited, there was no doubt that the Germans would destroy
us all.

In the meantime, some unexpected news reached me. One
day, I was working alongside a gentile girl named Zenia. She
started to talk to me and commented, "Do you know, there was a

girl of about your age who hid with my neighbors."

"Of my age? What was her name?"

"Marilka, I think."

"Marilka!" I said, excitedly. "What did she look like?"

When Zenia described the girl, it became clear that she was speaking of my cousin Marilka Finkelstein, my childhood friend. Glancing at the guard, I drew closer to Zenia and asked, "What

The check called "revisia"

happened to Marilka? Where is she now?"

"At the time of the *aktion*," replied Zenia, "Marilka's parents asked my gentile neighbor to take care of her until the storm blew over. She didn't look Jewish so it was no problem to hide her in a place where they weren't known. Marilka's parents, like many others, thought that the great danger was only to children and that young adults like themselves would be sent for a while to work camps, and eventually return to claim their children. Marilka waited several days without getting any news of her parents and began to worry. She left my neighbor's house and went to the ghetto to see what had happened to them. She didn't find her parents there, but could no longer leave the ghetto and was deported to Treblinka with the rest of the Jews."

The guard came up to me and cried: "Stop talking! You stand over there!" But I no longer had any desire to carry on the conversation...I had heard enough.

In my mind's eye I saw the lovely apartment which I had "cleaned" three months earlier. I saw Marilka's tidy things, her pretty clothes, her father's huge library, the violin that they had loved so much to play. And it was I who had packed that violin and all the rest of the family's possessions, in an orderly fashion, so that the Germans could more easily take them.... I would never see Marilka again...so gifted, so accomplished...and only thirteen years old....

*   *   *

Amidst all this, the snows began to melt and water dripped from the roofs. At first it just dirtied the blanket of white until it was quite grey, but slowly, the snow grew thinner and thinner until only a few patches remained here and there. The skies began to clear, hinting that spring was truly on its way.

Mother decided to tidy the "house" for the approaching Pesach (Passover).[1] At night, my mother, sisters, and I would scrub,

1. At Pesach it is customary in Jewish homes to thoroughly clean the

clean, and tidy our room from top to bottom. It wasn't easy. We slaved fourteen hours a day, seven days a week, away from the house. At the end of a long, exhausting work day we were worn out. Even so, we took it upon ourselves to clean our living quarters thoroughly in honor of Pesach, as we had traditionally done in happier times. We also decided not to bring *chametz* (leaven) into the house,[2] even though this meant that our already limited diet would be restricted even more. "Pesach is the festival of freedom," I said to myself. "Perhaps God will help us, too, and as He took our fathers out of Egypt with a mighty hand an outstretched arm, perhaps He will lead us, too, out to freedom."

When the Seder[3] night came, we sat down at a set table. Only one thing was available in abundance — the bitter herbs. We wanted to begin by reading the Haggadah,[4] and instead of reciting "Why is this night different from all other nights?" we all burst into tears of anguish at seeing Father's empty chair. Was he, too, celebrating Pesach? With whom? In what company? We overcame our sadness and continued to read the Haggadah. Tomorrow we must once again get up for roll call and go to work.

That Pesach we ate only one meal a day, usually potato soup.

---

house from top to bottom so that no crumbs of bread remain. Pesach stands out among other festivals of the Jewish year not only for the complex and elaborate rituals which accompany it but also, and primarily, for its celebration of the Exodus, the central event of the Jewish historical and religious experience.

2. During the Exodus from Egypt the children of Israel did not have time to permit the bread to rise, and their hasty departure is recalled by eating only unleavened bread during the seven days of the festival. For those days, all food containing leaven or yeast, and all fermented food products, are banned.

3. The traditional Pesach meal, at which the story of the Exodus is recited and symbolically re-experienced.

4. Literally the "recitation" or "retelling" of the Exodus from Egypt. A formal text is used, often handsomely illustrated, and this is also known as the "Haggadah."

The rest of the time we fasted. It was hard to watch the other girls eating bread and to refrain...but I reminded myself that in the bunker, there hadn't even been potato soup, and I hadn't given way there. "Never mind," I thought, "no one dies from fasting like this." I remembered the saying of the Fathers in the Talmud: "Who is strong? He who overcomes his (evil) impulse." Now I understood that saying only too well.

After not passing the selection, these people are being taking to death...

Chapter Twenty-four

The Revolt

Some people were sent to the same place of work each day. I, to my regret, was not so lucky. Everywhere I went, I was rejected because of my youth. For this reason, I was forced to look for a new job every day. Often, when I did not manage to find work, I would slip back into the ghetto and hide there with my little brothers until the family returned from work. Work was a kind of "license to live" which entitled one to a ration of food.

Many of the jobs were temporary, lasting only a few days, sometimes only one or two. One such task was "cleaning" Jewish homes — removing their entire contents and readying them for dispatch. This work went on for a relatively short period. Often, a number of girls would be given household chores in German homes. The Germans would often give parties and would afterwards need help washing the dirty dishes and putting the apartment in order.

Together with a large group of other girls, about fifty of us in all, I was given work in large field. After the German occupation, many of the Polish farmers had been sent to work in Germany, and they left behind them fertile lands near Czenstochow which were not being worked for lack of labor. The Germans expropriated these lands from their absent owners and brought groups of people from the ghetto to work them. To my good fortune, I too was included in this group.

*   *   *

May, 1943. For several weeks I worked with my sister Rivka preparing the field for sowing. I was very happy to be able to work in the fresh air and to enjoy the soft caress of the warm sunshine, which made my fair hair fairer still. With a heavy hoe, I turned over the clods of rich brown soil, under the supervision of an elderly Pole. Next to me worked Franka, a young woman of about twenty-three, large and plump. Her good-heartedness was revealed in the smile which never left her lips. She worked with exceptional speed, and her hoe cut through the hard ground as if it were butter. She advanced with great strides over the patch of ground assigned to her.

For me, the iron hoe was extremely heavy, and I could hardly manage to lift it. When Franka saw that I was moving forward at a snail's pace and that the distance between us was growing greater and greater, she began to fear that the old Pole would hit me. So whenever he moved off to supervise other girls, she would change places with me, and by the time he got back to us she had closed the gap between her row and mine, even overtaking me.

Now, working alongside me, Franka told me that she belonged to a group of partisans and hoped soon to leave the ghetto and hide in the forests in order to actively fight the Germans. She was very open with me and showed incredible trust in me by telling me all these stories. After all, I was only fourteen.

Rysia, nicknamed one-toothed Rysia, also worked with us. She was younger than Franka, only about twenty. One day, she had been beaten up by a German, and as a result, all her front teeth, except one, were broken — which is how she got her nickname.

This Rysia became very friendly with Franka, and she, too, decided to join the partisans. Indeed, after several days, the two disappeared from the horizon and were not seen again.

In the meantime, we got information that an armed revolt had broken out in the Warsaw ghetto. This revolt lasted six

View of the Warsaw ghetto after the revolt

weeks. The father of my uncle, the Gaon of Praga, Rabbi Menachem Ziemba, was the spiritual leader of the revolt. He was killed by German bullets, and some of his friends buried him deep in the earth, placing a note bearing his name into the grave. After the war, his burial place was accidentally discovered by workers digging at the site. When his friends learned of this, they brought the body to Israel, and he is now buried in Jerusalem.

At the end of May, 1943, the Warsaw ghetto was liquidated.

*   *   *

June 21, 1943. That day I presented myself for work at the Rakov factory with my sister Rivka. When we came back to the ghetto at the end of the day, we were all thoroughly searched. The Germans were more cruel than usual. They even searched our bodies, and only after they failed to find anything at all were we allowed into the ghetto.

As we stood in the marketplace, the sound of singing suddenly blared out from the big building that served as the command post of the German and Ukrainian police. The song grew louder and louder. It came from the lips of young men who had recently learned it:

> *"Treblinka dort*
> *Fahr yeden yid a gutten ohrt*
> *Vehr fohrt an hien farbliebt schoen dohrt*
> *farbliebt of abieg."*

("Treblinka, that's a good place for every Jew.
Whoever goes there remains,
remains there forever.")

The words of this new song pierced deep into my heart, and I felt its meaning with every fiber of my being. I, too, had family in that "good place"....

The atmosphere in the marketplace was full of tension, more so than usual. We felt that something terrible was about to happen. Something dreadful was in store for us.

We went into the ghetto. People, sad and downcast, told us that arrests had been made. The same fellow who had escaped from Treblinka had managed to organize some of the youngsters to revolt. They had even managed to get hold of a few rifles and some explosives, and the uprising was planned for a few days hence. In the midst of all this, one of the youths was arrested. He attempted to resist and, in the process, killed a German. He, in turn, was killed on the spot, and with him several young bystanders. The atmosphere was now unbearably tense.

"What should we do?" asked young neighbors.

"Perhaps we should hide?"

"Who knows what tomorrow will bring?"

Broken and despondent to the depth of our hearts, we separated from the others and went home to sleep. At least we could lie down for a few hours to gather strength to face the troubles that the cursed Nazis were preparing for us.

The next day, June 22, I again joined a group of workers at the Rakov factory, together with my sister Rivka. During roll call, Mr. Glicksman, the Jewish foreman, came up to us and instructed me to leave. "You are young and cannot work like an adult," he explained.

"Have pity on her, Mr. Glicksman," begged Rivka. "The ghetto is so tense, and the Germans are raging and fuming, full of murderous rage."

"All right," he replied, "but only this once. If you show yourself here again as part of the work group, I'm turning you over to the Germans."

"Thank you, Mr. Glicksman," I said, thinking in my heart: "By tomorrow God will help me from another source...in the ghetto, who knows what each day will bring."

Later, Mr. Glicksman came over to my sister and apologized. "I simply have no choice," he said. "If the German himself points her out as being too young, it will be even worse."

Chapter Twenty-five
A Pall of Smoke over the Ghetto

That day, I had bought a kilo of hard white cheese from a gentile woman. I paid her five zlotys — all the money that Rivka and I had. I planned to sell the cheese that night in the ghetto and buy some bread for our little brothers with the proceeds. The "illegals" did not get their own bread rations. Each one of us gave a quarter of our own ration and the rest melted in the mouth like candy. Our stomachs always "played" a symphony of hunger.

At the end of a hard day's work, we had to arrange our tools in perfect order, in a fixed place. The German supervisor would leisurely check them, and if there was even the slightest disorder, he would punish us with murderous blows.

When this check was uneventfully completed, we would arrange ourselves in rows of six; six men, six women, and thus march out of the factory gate. Here we were counted once again by five more Germans.

On this occasion, the gate did not open as usual at the end of the count, and one of the Germans told us: "From today onwards you will stay here at Rakov. You are not going back to the ghetto. The ghetto is booby-trapped and will soon be set on

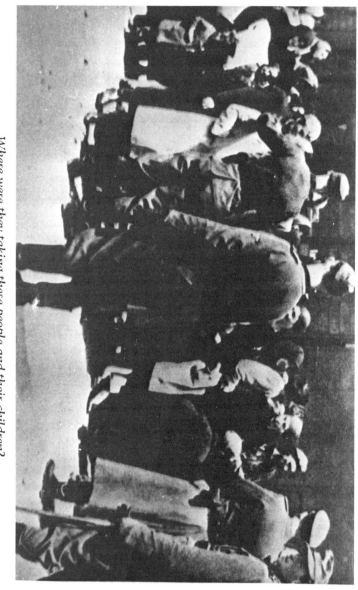

Where were they taking these people and their children?

fire.... You should thank me for saving you from being burned alive there."

This announcement struck us like thunder on a clear day. It had never occurred to us, even for a moment, that we would not go back to the ghetto, to our beloved families. Most of us had relatives there who worked in other places. Thoughts dashed through my mind and the words stuck in my throat — what would happen to our mother? It was a Thursday, the day on which she often stayed home to prepare at least something for Shabbat. And where were Chanoch and Yisroelik?

While we stood there, petrified with shock, the order was given in German: "Forward! To the dormitories!"

Mr. Glicksman, who stood as if nailed to the floor, recovered first. He raised first one leg as if it didn't belong to him, then the other, and moved forward. The German pointed to two sheds at the edge of the factory: one for men, one for women. He then turned and left us.

As if part of a great funeral procession, we began to walk towards the sheds, with spinning heads and wet eyes. From time to time, deep cries and groans burst from our broken hearts. I felt as if all my tears had dried up. I walked alongside Rivka in great misery.

When we reached the shed, each one of us was given a bit of straw to spread on the ground for a bed. We sat and looked at the setting sun; a large golden ball in the sky, growing redder and redder until it disappeared from sight, as if sending us a last farewell from our loved ones.... After that, total darkness. The heavens were bare, devoid of stars. All was extinguished. I moved closer to Rivka and held her hand in both of mine. As long as she didn't leave me...as long as I didn't lose her....

My sister understood what I was feeling and hugged me. We were all completely worn out with fatigue.

We lay down without uttering a word. From time to time a sigh broke out, unable to be suppressed any longer. I suddenly felt hot tears on my hand, flowing from the eyes of one of the girls, my neighbor in the shed who lay next to me.

Some time after midnight, a mighty explosion was heard. We leaped to our feet and rushed outside. From the direction of the small ghetto, we saw huge tongues of flame and clouds of smoke spread out over the area of the three streets. The skies were lit by a brilliant red light, as if thousands of electric bulbs had been switched on. Awful screams burst from the lips of the girls, like wounded beasts. Where are our dear ones now?

For a long time we stood there, staring at that horrible scene. We shivered from cold, though it was a mild summer night. A chill spread through our insides, as if we had turned to ice. I moved up to my sister Rivka in total, stupefied silence. The heart spoke its own language, weeping blood, flowing inwards, into my body....

None of us managed to sleep again that night, despite our great exhaustion. Our misery and fear gave us no rest. Then a girl named Henya Gold, aged eighteen, one of four sisters, broke out in sad song, about, of all things, a Chinese geisha girl. Her rich voice, full of feeling, took a bit of our sadness to another land, to China, distant, poor, hungry, and sad.

Thus, this night too ended. And, strangely, the sun's rays peeping into the open shed smiled as if nothing had changed since the beginning of time. As on other days, we had to get up for roll call, only today we did not come from the ghetto. We met at the iron gate of the factory. Right on time. Heaven forbid that we should antagonize the Germans now.

Many Polish gentiles worked at Rakov for a weekly wage. They began work early, while we were still standing at roll call. From them we learned a little about what had happened in the ghetto the previous night. "The Germans sealed off the ghetto; we saw the blaze," they said. Some even commiserated with us in our sorrow. Others added, "It was in revenge for the attempt to revolt that the Germans booby-trapped the ghetto and set fire to it in the night."

We were also told that a few hours before the explosion, the Germans sent Jewish emissaries to the ghetto to try to persuade those in hiding to come out and save themselves from the fire. It was all amazingly well organized and well planned. Indeed, the precision, the discipline, the order, were astounding.

Thoughts of my dear ones gave no rest: Had they been saved? Had they left the ghetto and hidden themselves somewhere? Mr. Glicksman, our foreman, tried in vain to find out more details of what had happened. We were cut off from our world. Everything blended together into a deep, grey fog.

Chapter Twenty-six

My Mother's Wedding Ring

Three weeks after these events we received a letter from our sisters at the Hasag factory, smuggled in to us by a Pole working at Hasag, whose sister-in-law worked at Rakov. We read it with bated breath; a sign of life from our family!

With joy we read that our oldest sister, Hela, was at Hasag together with her husband and our two other sisters. "Chanoch was brought to us after the burning of the ghetto," wrote the sisters. "It is a great miracle that he survived." We immediately noted that there was no mention of our mother or Yisroelik, and our anxiety increased.

By means of the same channel we wrote a note of reply, asking for full details about our mother and brother.

*　　　*　　　*

It should be recalled that my goods for petty trading were still with me on the night the ghetto burned — a kilo of white cheese that I had bought for five zlotys, our last money. I divided the piece of cheese into six portions, and sold each slice for one zloty. I also bought foodstuffs from one of the gentile women who worked with us, and sold them to others. This trade paid off; the gentile woman was honest and never let me down. Thus, Rivka and I were provided with "luxuries," additions to our rations, and we were even able to send a few zlotys to the Hasag.

It was two months before another letter arrived and we could find out what had happened to Mother and Yisroelik.

That same Thursday, June 22, 1943, in the morning, the Germans announced over the loudspeaker that all the inhabitants of the ghetto were to assemble in the marketplace within the hour.

"Whoever does not come out will be burned alive! The ghetto is booby-trapped."

Even the patients in the small hospital left their beds and came to the marketplace. There was even a new mother there — the only one in the ghetto — who left her lying-in and came. She was sent to work at Hasag.

Our beloved mother left our room with the two boys and went to the marketplace. Chanoch stood on a stone — perhaps this would make him look taller and more grown-up, more fit for work. Yisroelik stood next to Mother and looked around him. He noticed that the Germans had brought several trucks to the market and were throwing children into them. They caught them by the hands or feet, and threw them one after the other into the trucks, as if they were dummies, and not children of flesh and blood.

"Mama," said Yisroelik. "Come back to the ghetto with me. They are throwing children around like packages. They want to kill them!"

"You are right," said Mother with pale lips. She forgot herself and gave up her chance to escape. She took Yisroelik by the hand, and they went back to the ghetto. The Germans finished "collecting" the youngsters and began to search among the grown-ups; perhaps a child was hiding there, a terrible enemy, dangerous to the Reich.... They found about twenty children standing with their parents, among them Chanoch, whose young face (he was, after all, only eleven years old) gave him away, even though he was standing on a stone.

The last group of children were taken to the Jewish cemetery. On the way, the manager of Hasag, a German by the name of Litt, passed by and saw the truck full of ten to thirteen year-olds.

"Where are you taking those children?" he asked.

"To the Jewish cemetery," was the reply.

"Such big kids? I object. Bring them to Hasag. They can be put to some use there."

Thus Chanoch was saved from death by a miracle — although for most of those children, this proved only a short respite. About ten days later there was another selection at Hasag, and some ten children and dozens of adults were sent to Treblinka. A month later there was another selection, and five children together with adults were sent off.... Thus there remained only five children in Hasag at its closure on January 16, 1945, when the Germans transferred the workers, ourselves among them, to Germany. Of these five children, only three remained alive, including our Chanoch.

In the meantime, Mother and Yisroelik hid in a bunker. When the Germans, with characteristic thoroughness, had completed their "purification" of humans from the marketplace, they sent messengers back to the ghetto with loudspeakers.

"Whoever comes out within the hour," they declared, "will be given amnesty and sent to work at the Hasag factory."

Mother, in her innocence, came out of the bunker with Yisroelik and a group of about forty other people. Under heavy guard they were taken to the suburb where Hasag was situated.

"We saw a group of Jews," recounted some Poles, "with an armed German guard." Our beloved mother and our little brother Yisroelik were in that group. Mother took off her wedding ring and asked a gentile woman to give it to her daughters, whose family name is Dziubas, from their mother. I don't know how she managed to do this under the noses of the guard. But the gentile woman did indeed bring the ring to my sisters, with a little note hidden in it: "Say Kaddish for me."

"Half an hour later," the gentiles related, "the whole group was put onto a truck and taken to the cemetery. The men dug a large grave and the Germans shot them all — down to the very last one.

"How these monsters called 'humans' could shoot parents with their children like that, we just cannot understand," said the Poles who witnessed the massacre.

Appell

Chapter Twenty-seven
At the Rakov Factory

L ife went on even after the disaster. The days passed and it was already August. During our work at this iron-processing factory, a long and backbreaking job, we saw the sun here and there, the blue of the skies, and even the tops of green trees. Beside the railway wagons we were made to load, I could discern the beauty of these color combinations.

At the Rakov factory there was an iron-smelting furnace. We filled the wagons with iron ore and then with coal and lime. From the combinations of coal and ore smelted at very high temperatures, iron is produced. The furnace was heated to 1539° C. The iron was separated from the dross, which was drained out by a special pipe.

Three kinds of iron were produced at the factory — cast iron, blacksmiths' iron, and steel.

Cast iron was produced directly from the furnace. By means of rapid cooling, white cast iron was produced. This was a brittle metal with a crude lumpy structure. When the cooling process is slower, a great deal of carbon evaporates, producing grey cast iron. Because of the low cutting temperature, 300° C, and because of its tendency to spread when it is solid, this iron is used as casting material from which great quantities of tools and implements of all kinds were cast.

Some of the iron underwent further processing to become

nickel — rustproof iron.

The furnace was never extinguished, but burned constantly, because producing the high temperatures required took two weeks. At night, I would sometimes wander around near the factory. There were mounds of gleaming snow, marked by the giant snakelike slash of red — the leavings from the iron which were tipped out onto the piles like boiling lava. It was a splendid sight, the red "snake" gleaming in the darkness, climbing among the snows and descending to the valleys.

Apart from iron ore, we loaded the wagons also with scrap-iron, among which we sometimes found real treasures: a whole pot, or a frying pan, in which we would try to prepare something for Shabbat from the goods we managed to obtain through our trading.

Meanwhile, we had been moved from the sheds to huts which were erected for our use. Each one of us got her permanent place for the night, a "territory" of about 1.8 meters long and 60 centimeters wide — the size of a grave! Nonetheless, I was content to have a "fixed address" of my own, together with my sister Rivka.

I was the only young girl at the factory, and the Polish workers had pity on me. "She doesn't look like a laborer, that little one, but like a princess," they said. Each day I would find a sandwich that someone had left for me. They knew that I wouldn't take anything from anyone, and chose this delicate way of helping me fight off starvation.

At first I felt very strange at work, and was hesitant to look anyone directly in the eye. I was frightened and didn't know the people. Yet, these simple folk interpreted my behavior correctly.

Indeed, I was little more than a child — and would sometimes forget myself and laugh or sing. Thus, I reminded the Jews of their own children, or of the little sisters whose fate they knew not. And thus, they would often spoil me with some delicacy or a slice of bread.

I would soothe myself by thinking, "This is only a temporary situation. Soon, in a few days or a couple of weeks, all this
will end, with God's help, and we will return home to my parents, brothers, and sisters."

In this way I strengthened myself and happily pushed away
the sorrows and suffering of the present. "If we can only hold out
and overcome our pain, God will help us and save us." I trusted in
this with all my heart.

The summer passed, and in its place came strong winds and
heavy rains. The heavens were grey, covered with leaden clouds.
The few trees at Rakov were stripped naked; only a few leaves still
clung to them here and there. A thick carpet of golden brown and
yellow leaves covered the ground. Only a year ago I had collected
leaves like these for a nature lesson, together with my friends on
the avenue. Now, the wind scattered the leaves in all directions,
and there were no more children to gather them.

I was aroused from these sad thoughts by a shout. "Forward
march, to work!" Hastily, I suppressed my reflections. To work,
before the gentile overseer showered me with blows; perhaps tomorrow I would have time to think, or the day after....

An unpleasant incident took place during these days. There
was a woman who frequently made unfriendly remarks to me,
and one day I responded to these with a very ugly word. The
woman complained to Rivka, who got angry and slapped me. I
was deeply hurt, although the slap was not hard, because all this
had taken place in front of the woman herself and several other
people. As I have said, I was spoiled by everyone and was used to
special treatment. I cried a lot that evening and could not look
my sister in the face.

"Rutka, why are you crying?"

I didn't answer Rivka, nor did I turn my head.

"Because of that slap?"

I only cried harder.

"I'm sorry Rutka. It was a spontaneous reaction. Please forgive me. It's true. I really have no right. After all, I am not your mother. Come on, let's forget it. It's all over and done with."

"Forgotten."

And so, even these little things could still hurt. A sign that I was not, after all, deeply changed. That, too, was a good thing.

Chapter Twenty-eight

At the Hasag Factory

One day, a certain gentile suggested to Rivka that he hide the two of us until the end of the war. A few days later we got another offer, from a different gentile, via one of the Jews who worked with us. He offered to get us "gentile papers," so we could live among Aryans.

"What do you think, Rutka?" asked Rivka. "Are you willing to accept one of these offers?"

"I don't know. It's really a difficult decision. Here, we are together with Jews, just like one large family."

"On the other hand, who knows what the Germans will decide to do to us tomorrow?"

"You're right — here we are slaves, just as our forefathers were to Pharaoh in Egypt. Let's think it over."

We delayed our answer and, meanwhile, conditions changed. The Germans decided that more women were needed to work at the Hasag factory. According to the decision, twenty women were to be transferred. This time we believed that the transfer was actually taking place (and was not just a cover for another *aktion*) because we had heard from some of the gentile workers that there was a shortage of hands at Hasag. Our sisters and brother Chanoch were there, and we longed to be reunited with them. However, there was also a certain fear of change. At Rakov, we had gotten used to the conditions, managed to acquire additional rations, and even saved a few zlotys. At all events, it was not our decision anyway, so that when we were informed of our transfer we were quite pleased.

In February of 1944, we were put onto a truck and taken to the Hasag factory. Here we were reunited with our sisters, Chanoch, and our brother-in-law, and we enjoyed a short hour of contentment.

However, all too soon, we were put to work under the ever-watchful eye of the Germans. Only at night, before the general "lights out," could we chat a little and tell each other about our experiences over the last months.

Each morning at 6:00 A.M., a roll call was held which lasted about one hour, and only after that did we go to work. Each one had his special task. Hasag had been converted by the Germans into a huge ammunition factory. The many machines worked twenty-three hours a day, with a break of thirty minutes twice daily. During this half hour, we received a portion of soup and went to the bathroom. Huge lines formed outside the two places which were both so vital to us. More than once I debated with myself which was more essential, food or relief, and which of the lines I should join.

During working hours it was forbidden to go to the bathroom unless you had a substitute — and there was only one "substitute" for several dozen girls.

My job was sorting bullets. I had to check them to see if the machine had correctly sorted them according to their length and thickness, and also weighed them. The bullets were made out of yellow copper, and they had to be handled with soft white gloves. Two gentile technicians stood ready to repair the machines whenever necessary. During the twelve-hour shift, except for the half-hour break, we were forbidden to remove our gaze from the machines.

As I worked at my task of sorting, all sorts of questions passed unceasingly through my mind: Where were these bullets being sent? Against whom were they being used? Against our brothers, the Jews? A shudder passed through my body.

"Don't think!" I told myself. "Just work!"

When we lay down exhausted at night, we sometimes discussed this problem. But what could we do? We had no choice. Our hearts ached, but to no avail.

Chapter Twenty-nine

Pesach

That winter was a hard and bitterly cold one. The cold penetrated our hut, and I was glad that we slept close together and in this way managed to keep warm.

When I returned from washing after work, my hair was full of little lumps of ice, from the water which had clung to my head. Even so, I thanked God that I had water and soap and the possibility of washing myself clean — not like in the bunker.

The days were dark and grey. The sun was scarcely seen. In fact, there hardly seemed to be any daylight at all. When we left for work on the night shift, we left in darkness and returned in the dim first light of morning. On the day shift we left in the morning before it was fully light and returned after sunset, in darkness.

More than once, I felt that we were living in a kind of perpetual night. Once more, there was no day, no sunshine. All was extinguished.

On these dark days I would pull from my heart pleasant and warming memories, without anyone noticing. I also had books to read. My sister, who worked in the manager's garden, often provided me with classic books by well-known writers. When I worked nights I would spend the day reading instead of sleeping. All my senses focused on this pastime. Many of the books told of the Scandinavian countries, Sweden and Norway. There were descriptions of the wonders of nature, of long nights and endless days on which the sun never set at all. Thus, by simply turning the page, I could pass into another, happier world.

Snow fell and covered the roofs of the huts. The few trees which stood in a line at the factory were wrapped in white. Everything looked like a wedding day. How lovely the white flakes were as they danced lightly on the air, in their rhythmic spirals and delicate fall to earth. In the good days, we had thrown snowballs at each other and would fly home from school on skates. Now, no one took any notice of the snow. Its beauty was concealed from their suffering eyes.

And we were hungry. The single slice of bread which was our daily ration fell to the pit of the stomach and disappeared there without leaving any impression whatsoever. Here we had no money and neither did anyone else. We had to rely on the rations distributed to us.

My sister made a dress for a gentile woman. She worked hard, sewing it entirely by hand. In payment she received only two loaves of bread. She gave them to my oldest sister, Hela, to distribute among all the members of our family. In this way, at the cost of my sister's sleep, we all enjoyed a substantial addition to our meager diet.

Often, my sister would bring a tomato or an onion from the camp manager's garden, which would revive us. Although this was her own daily ration that she received from the manager, she wouldn't even take a taste, but would smuggle the vegetables under her apron into the camp to share with us.

*　　*　　*

March, 1944. The snows melted and the fields turned into "lakes." Here and there something green peeped out of the soil. The trees, too, began to awaken from their winter slumber. One of the gentiles came to work with a flower in the lapel of her coat. It was wonderful to see the first flowers peeping through the snow — sweetly scented, purple blossoms which gladdened the

The Hasag Camp

heart. Children from the nearby villages used to sell them at street corners.

Even we, the slave laborers of Hasag, living most of our lives in darkness, could feel the approach of spring. Once again, I was filled with hope: tomorrow would be better, with God's help.

Pesach was almost with us. Until now, during the first four years of the war, we had kept the dietary laws of Pesach and eaten no leaven. This year, too, we tried to organize something, so that we might maintain our observance. We were even prepared to fast if necessary.

With our last pennies, we bought some beans and decided to cook for the whole of Pesach week. "Cooking" at Hasag was no simple matter. First of all, only girls who worked on the night shift could do this, because only during the day could a fire be lit without danger of discovery. The cooking was done over a "grate" made up of two bricks with a few branches of wood between them. The fire we made was full of soot, which somehow penetrated the pot and gave a deep color — and even a special flavor — to the contents. We wanted to cook the beans until they were at least soft enough to be eaten without suffering stomach pains.

On the first and second days of Pesach — the two days of the festival — we ate ordinary beans, albeit a little sooty. On the third and fourth days, the first and second of the intervening days of the festival, we were already eating "pickled" beans, and by the fifth day, the brew was already "meaty" — full of worms and quite spoiled. Therefore, for the last three days we ate only the potato soup distributed at the factory and went hungry. We couldn't accept the idea of eating leaven on Pesach, not even young Chanoch.

Spring was at its height and the fresh smell of the fields reached us even in the factory. My longing to see the blue skies became an imperative. I decided to make an effort to get a "substitute" and go out to the bathroom. My luck was good, for I managed to find one, and swift as an arrow from a bowstring, I shot outside.

The river Warta flowed near Hasag, and one of its small tributaries passed right by the area of the factory. Moist green grass grew near the river. I ran towards the river with all my might, threw off my shoes, and sat on the grass, paddling my feet in the cold water, enjoying the effect, which looked, to my eyes, like a work of art, painted gold on a blue and green background. Fluffy white clouds floated in the sky, and a little butterfly had made himself a swing out of a flower. There were red poppies and little yellow flowers, and the sun stood, all gold, in its full splendor. A cry of joy burst from my heart: "Master of the Universe! How beautiful is the world which You created! When will we, too, be able to enjoy its splendor?"

I awoke suddenly from my pleasant dream. Everything around was so beautiful — an island of delight, an island of loveliness. I felt as if new blood had been pumped into my veins and all the cells of my brain and body were refreshed by new hopes. All of this lasted only about ten minutes, but it left me with the feeling that I had enjoyed several hours in the bosom of nature. I hastened to put on my shoes, and ran back to the factory.

For a long time afterwards, I was encouraged by the memory of those wonderful moments that I spent on the bank of the river. In my most difficult hours, these moments helped me to remember that God lives eternally and that He would help me.

Chapter Thirty

The Transport from Pietrkow

I returned to the big hall, grey and cold, full of machines, copper, and bullets. The bullets were packed in boxes and chests and stacked along the walls in perfect order, ready to be loaded on the trucks that came each day to take the boxes to the front.

Weeks passed. From the Poles who worked with us, rumors filtered through about the campaign that the Allies, led by the United States, were starting against Germany. In June, 1944, there was talk of attempts to bomb Auschwitz, or at least the railway tracks that led there. There was another rumor that, already in April of that year, two people had escaped from the camp with precise plans of its layout. The plans were transmitted to Britain, the United States, and Switzerland. Millions had already been murdered by the Germans at Auschwitz, but the English evaded the issue, claiming that there were technical difficulties involved in carrying out bombing attacks. There was also a lack of sufficient awareness among Jews abroad who might otherwise have effectively lobbied for the bombing.

The Germans, hearing of their own failures on the various fronts, became even more cruel and vicious.

*   *   *

It was already the beginning of July, 1944. One day, a transport of people arrived from Pietrkow. I wanted to know who the

newcomers were, and so when I finished work at 7:00 P.M. I went
to the hall where the new arrivals were stationed. Perhaps there
would be girls of my own age among them, even if only one. And
perhaps we would hear news of our relatives!

These were the long days of summer, and it was still daylight
outside. I hastened to the small building which housed the new
arrivals. In the great hall with its 200 beds I found about 150 people: men and women, exhausted, hungry, and very frightened.
They had already managed to ascertain that Hasag was a work
camp (not a death camp) and that here they would remain.

Each person had a small bundle in his hand — all his
worldly belongings. We, the "old-timers," encouraged them by
telling them about the camp and its conditions which, relatively
speaking, were not bad. We knew that the Germans needed our
labor and that they therefore had to provide the minimum to ensure our survival.

"It's true there's not much to eat," we acknowledged, "and
there are beatings if the work isn't up to the requirements of the
Germans in charge of us. But, fortunately, there has been no selection here for months, and no one has been sent to the death
camps."

For their part, the people of Pietrkow told hair-raising stories
about their deportation, about Auschwitz, Majdanek, and Treblinka. "We are almost the only survivors of Pietrkow," they told
us. Pietrkow was a large town with thousands of Jews.

I wandered among the people, and suddenly my eye fell on
a sweet girl of about fourteen, dark-haired and pretty. I immediately went up to her.

"Hello! My name is Rutka. Can I ask what's yours?"

"Oh! Hello! I'm Dinka."

We sat on the steps of the building and began to talk. How
my spirits rose with this heart-to-heart chat! We talked about
books we had read and recalled characters from different stories.
We were happy to have the opportunity to talk like two young

friends, and not like depressed adults.

The sun set, and night fell. Reluctantly, I got to my feet. "I must go back to my hut," I said.

"So soon?" asked Dinka, disappointed.

"Never mind. We'll see each other again tomorrow," I promised, and ran to the huts. I sang to myself and hummed some favorite tunes; I was so happy to meet another girl of my own age!

"It is possible!" I said to myself. "The war will end and I will have friends again. I must be patient and God will help me and all of us."

Our huts were on the grounds of the factory and spread over a large area. There were five huts in all, two for women and three for men. They were surrounded by a high fence, and the entrance was through an iron gate. Jewish police stood near the gate by day and by night to prevent strangers from entering. From time to time we were "honored" by a visit from the Germans in charge of the Hasag factory.

It was already 9:30 and "lights out" was at 10:00. On the way to my hut, I received many quizzical glances. As I passed through the gate, my lips full of song, the police said nothing, but looked at me in astonishment: "How is it possible," they must have thought in their hearts, "to sing and smile in a place like this?"

In fact, the common mood was one of despondency, with people existing in a kind of haze, not knowing what had befallen their loved ones or what each new day would bring.

But at that moment, I was in good spirits and I continued to sing and chuckle as I entered the hut. Here, I felt, it was permissible to express my feelings and share them with others. But to my great amazement, I met only a strange silence. "Odd," I thought, "why doesn't anyone ask why I'm so cheerful?"

I looked around me; all faces were strained and distorted with anxiety. A moment later I heard a shout in German.

"Who dared to laugh? Bring her here!" was the order to the Jewish police. Without hesitation, I climbed to the third level of our bunks and from them crawled on all fours to some of the other beds.

"Who laughed?" demanded the little German, Stieglitz, and he roared in rage when he got no answer. He grabbed two girls as "hostages" and screamed at the top of his voice:

"If you don't tell me immediately who laughed, I'll kill you both!"

And then the unfortunate girls pointed at me.

"Hold her!" barked the German to the Jewish police. Now a chase started. I skipped from bed to bed, until after a few minutes, my right leg got caught in a crack between the beds. I understood that there was no point in further resistance. The Jewish policeman dragged me off the bed and handed me over to the German, whose face resembled a monkey's. He looked at me with his small eyes, full of murder, and shrieked, "Out!" Then with his rifle butt he pushed me forward, out of the hut.

"I'm lost," I thought. "I had better say *Shema Yisrael....*"

Chapter Thirty-one

A Gun at My Head

Outside, a large moon lit the dark skies. The repulsive and ugly Stieglitz stood and looked at me. Then he took from his holster a small, shiny, black revolver and pointed it at me.

"Why did you laugh?" he asked in German.

"He'll finish me off, he'll kill me," I thought. He was tense and angry; apparently he thought I had been laughing at him.

I drew myself upright and decided: "I won't be afraid! He can only kill my body. My spirit will return, pure, to its Maker...."

"I didn't laugh," I said in German.

"I'm asking you for the last time, why did you laugh?! Answer me!"

"I didn't laugh," I repeated firmly.

He stood looking at me. By the light of the moon he looked like a gorilla, straight out of the jungle. I prepared myself for death and asked God only that I might not suffer for very long. Suddenly, Stieglitz lowered the pistol and, with a hand of steel, slapped me across the face. I rocked with the force of the blows and was sure that he had broken my cheekbones. I forced myself to stand upright, supporting myself on the wall of the hut. I knew that if I fell he would tread on me with his feet, encased in their strong, nailed, leather boots. We all knew those boots well; woe to he who felt their weight on his flesh.

Stieglitz puffed and panted and cursed in rage, at the same time moving away from me.

I pulled myself together and staggered back into the hut. My sisters were overjoyed to see me, as were the two girls who had given me away. The poor things begged my forgiveness; everyone was afraid that I had been made to pay for my laughter with my life.

My cheeks were very swollen from the slaps and ached badly. My sisters wet a towel and held it to my face all through the night. Later that same night, Stieglitz, accompanied by the Jewish police, returned and warned us:

"Any girls who were 'honored' with beatings are required to report for work as usual!" He added, "Tomorrow I will conduct an inspection in this hut, and if I find an 'invalid' or someone who is 'unfit for work,' I will show her what 'unfit for work' really means!"

*   *   *

To my regret, my wonderful relationship with Dinka was soon cut off. The next day she was put on the night shift at the bullet-sorting machine, so that we almost never met.

At Hasag there were only two shifts of twelve hours each. There were no Shabbats, no holidays. We were forced to work seven days a week, without missing a day or an hour.

In the great hall where the machines ran day and night, there wasn't even a break between shifts. At 7:00, morning and evening, the incoming shift would enter the hall and each person would stand beside one of the outgoing shift, who still worked at his machine. When the signal was given, those finishing work would stand aside to enable those beginning the new shift to take their places with the minimum interruption of work. It was forbidden to talk. When the changeover was completed, the outgoing shift lined up and was counted and marched back to the hut for a short rest. At lunch time we received our soup ration and the hut was then filled with voices and chatter, so that it was almost impossible to sleep. In the afternoon we used to wash the clothes we wore; they were the only ones we possessed. We also took pains to maintain order and cleanliness in our hut. So it was that only rarely did I manage to exchange a hasty word with my friend Dinka. Deep in my heart I felt her presence and looked forward to the day when we could really get together and talk to our hearts' content.

*   *   *

In spite of everything, I did manage to escape somewhat from the harsh reality of life. My sister, who worked in the garden of Mr. Litt, the director of the camp, received books from the old gardener and brought them to me. One day she gave me the book *Kasper Hauser — Child of Europe*, by the German-Jewish writer Jakob Wasserman. This author's work took me away from the hunger and sadness of the Hasag camp. The book tells of a boy, the son of princes, who is kidnapped at the age of two or three and kept in a dark cellar until he grows up.

The boy lives in darkness, without light, without seeing human beings, without the sounds of nature. At night, food and drink is passed in to him. He grows up wild and doesn't even recognize human speech. He goes around on all fours like an animal. As I read I cried — I was so sorry for Kasper that my own troubles were forgotten. Since I was working the night shift, I could spend the whole day reading. However, this meant that I got no sleep at all during the day, and at night I had to present myself for a twelve-hour stretch of work, so that I did not close my eyes for thirty-six hours.

I was afraid that I would fall asleep on the job and be brutally beaten for it. To my good fortune, another girl agreed to change jobs with me. My usual job on the night shift was sitting and watching the "*augenschein*" — a kind of mirror through which the bullet cases were checked to see if they were all punched with two holes. I would certainly have dropped off to sleep at this boring task. Instead, I now had to load the bullet cases into the machine.

Loading the machines was done standing up, so that it was harder to doze off. Two German women, Marianna and Berta, checked the cases all the time. If they found something out of order the Ukrainian guard was called, and he took the "guilty" girl to the foreman's office where she was beaten with heavy leather straps. If she got ten blows her back was striped; if she got twenty she was marked with squares. We would see the colored markings on her back when we went to wash.

Chapter Thirty-two

The Transports from Lodz and Skarzysko

At the end of August, 1944, a new shipment of about 150 people arrived, this time from Lodz. They looked terrible — skin and bones, like skeletons. It was hard to look at these human shadows; their expressionless eyes stared out of their skulls and they were so weak, they could hardly speak.

They told us about their hard life in the Lodz ghetto, about the hunger, the epidemics, and death which lurked in every corner. Selections and deportations happened frequently, and there was no rest from the accursed Germans. Selections took place about every two weeks, and hundreds of people were sent "away"...adults, youths, and children. "Now," they told us, "the ghetto has been liquidated and everyone except us has been sent to Auschwitz."

As was their wont, the Germans had always told the Jews of Lodz that they were being sent to labor camps. The head of the Judenrat, Chaim Rumkowski, helped the Germans to carry out this task with their usual perfect order. He made available to them lists of all the Jews in the ghetto so that before each transport, the Germans had only to call out the names, condemning their bearers to life or death. Mr. Rumkowski did not know where the Jews were being sent, and when he did find out, it was too late....

There were factories in the Lodz ghetto for the production of footwear and clothing, and many Jews were employed there. These workers got special ration cards. People were willing to pay a great deal of money to be included among the factory workers, as they enjoyed a kind of immunity and were kept unharmed throughout the selections. Times were such that a simple cobbler could be raised to become manager of a shoe factory, or a tailor, manager of a clothes factory. These petty tradesmen thus became "high society" and everyone sought their favor.

Fortunately, most of them were goodhearted people who tried to help their Jewish brethren, although their opportunities to do so were extremely limited.

This was the experience of the Lodz ghetto during the war.

The newcomers brought us greetings from our dear mother's sisters, her brother-in-law, and her nephew, some of whom remained alive until the liquidation of the ghetto.

They brought with them good clothes and suits which they exchanged for bread and other foodstuffs. They were so hungry that they would stuff themselves with food and then vomit, as their stomachs were unused to large quantities of food.

The very next day, the Lodz contingent was put to work. One of the women worked alongside me, checking bullets. Suddenly she did something very strange. She took some of the black paste used to grease the machines and, before my astonished eyes, anointed her head and body with it.

"Why are you doing that?" I inquired, aghast.

"It's grease, right?"

"Right."

"Well, if it's grease, it's good for me. I feel a lack of grease and fat, I'm dehydrated, all dried up."

Then I realized how relatively good our conditions were at Hasag, where we were assured a daily bread ration and also a plate of hot soup.

The Jews from the Lodz ghetto

*   *   *

About a month later, another transport reached us, this time from Skarzysko, a small town which had a large ammunition factory, like Hasag. The Germans transported large, heavy machines together with the workers and vacated some of the halls at the factory to house them.

The Skarzysko Jews brought important news: "The Russians have bombed the town," they whispered. "The end of the war is coming...." But until that day of redemption, we still faced five very difficult months.

Some of the people of Skarzysko were distinguishable by their yellow faces and skin.

"That's because we worked with Cyclon," they explained.

"Cyclon?" we asked.

"It's a yellow poison in powder form which destroys human blood cells."

One of the men added, "In normal times, anyone working with Cyclon used to work only four hours a day, under special conditions, with plenty of leave, special food, and an extra ration of milk."

"But not the Jews," sighed another.

"For the Germans, the Jews are not human beings."

The Jews worked with Cyclon twelve hours a day, seven days a week, and their food was scarce and scanty. It was not surprising, therefore, that it was not long before they were completely destroyed.

"Haven't you heard of Block Three?"

"No, what's that?"

"That's our block, the punishment block. Whoever got on the wrong side of the Germans was sent to Block Three. From there, there was no return...people would become *musselmen*[5] and be sent to Auschwitz or Treblinka."

A sigh accompanied this conversation, and with good reason. The coming of the Skarzysko transport aroused once more

---

5.   Camp inmates who became totally passive and skeleton-like in appearance as a result of starvation and brutalization. Unable to defend themselves, they were the living dead.

the fear of deportation. Since a number of the machines that had been brought with the transport stood unused for lack of space, there was now a certain surplus of manpower. This problem could have only one solution — selection. There was talk of a work camp in Germany, but who could believe the Germans?

Tension reached its peak one morning, when, while we stood at roll call, the Germans appeared with lists in their hands.

The murmur passed: "They've brought lists...." Each one of us strengthened his stance to demonstrate his physical fitness.

"All those whose names are called," announced the Germans, "are to move to the right."

This time, about 200 people stepped to the right, including my brother-in-law and me. It was not unexpected; the German supervisor, Marianna, had had an eye on me for some time. I was too young, and my work output was not that of an adult. She would constantly harass me by standing over me for hours, not taking her eyes off my work, and endlessly moving me around from place to place.

My cousin Madzja, who had also been my teacher in the *komplet*, came to my aid. She pulled me out of the group by force and begged Marianna, "Please leave her alone."

This act took a lot of courage, even though Madzja was among the outstanding workers at the factory. Most probably, she simply didn't realize her own "chutzpah." At all events, thank God, I was allowed to remain at Hasag. That same morning, the others, including my brother-in-law, were sent to Germany. After an hour's wait, a truck arrived to take them off to the train. My sister Hela cried all night: she knew in her heart that she would never see her husband again.

Chapter Thirty-three

The Bombing of Czenstochow

December, 1944. It was the depths of winter and our hut was unbearably cold. The whole region was covered with a thick layer of snow. The glazed windows of the hut were covered in nature's art work: flowers drawn on the ice.

I was working with Marianna again, usually on the night shift. At 4:00 or 5:00 A.M. I would be waging a desperate war on my eyelids, so that they should not close from lack of sleep. The block was noisy during the daytime, and it was impossible to get more than four or five hours of sleep.

There was good news, too. The Russians were advancing and the bombing of German installations came nearer and nearer to Czenstochow. Perhaps soon we would be free. The Germans, once bitten, twice shy, had decided not to transfer us to Germany until the very last minute. They had erred in moving the Skarzysko contingent too soon and were now trying to slow down the transfer of machines and workers into Germany.

"Dear God, give us just a little more strength to hang on; perhaps we will soon be liberated, be free people once again...."

January, 1945. Rumor followed rumor. We had no radio and no newspapers, but there was a general feeling that something was about to happen. The Germans' behavior also changed. The senior officers went off to Germany. Marianna and Berta screamed and shouted in an attempt to maintain discipline and order, as before. Several of the Poles failed to show up for work, and the Germans insisted on bringing them in by force. Order, as is well known, must be maintained....

I smiled to myself when I remembered an anecdote that Marilka's father had told us. He was talking to a German officer who was showing off about Germany's conquests of territory, enumerating the large countries and important cities that had been occupied. Marilka's father asked him: "Have you already occupied '*A mitah meshunah*' (Hebrew for 'a strange death')?" The officer studied the list in his hand and said, "No, not yet, but of course we will soon have that, too!"

January 15. There was great tension at the factory. The Germans had begun to "lose their cool" for the first time and rushed around like poisoned rats. Nervously they tried to make contact with their command base and couldn't. All the telephone lines to Germany were busy. Discipline became very slack; many Poles were missing from work and those who did appear told us: "The Russians are coming! Only a few more days and Czenstochow will be free."

January 16, 1945. The Germans disconnected the main electricity supply at the factory and work ceased. They listened endlessly to the radio...several Germans disappeared and others began to pack. Some girls broke into the foodstore and one of the Jewish supervisors began to distribute all the food that came to hand. Bread, margarine, and sugar — our rations for a whole week. We also bundled up our few possessions and prepared food for the journey. We considered escaping, but when we asked "Where to?" we found no answer. It was freezing outside. Where could we hide?

We heard the noise of bomber planes over our town and from time to time the sound of exploding bombs falling not very far away. We couldn't bring ourselves to any practical decision; the Germans were few and the Jews many, but the Germans were also armed. Rumor had it that they would try at all costs to prevent the factory from falling into the hands of the Russians and would therefore set fire to it before they left. Others maintained that it was better to remain at the factory and hide there. Meanwhile two German officers came up and assembled us.

"We want to ask you to leave the factory with us," they said just as if they were actually talking to human beings. "We want to save you from death! If you come with us to the labor camp you will be well taken care of; we'll look after you."

Other Germans joined them from somewhere, and they, too, tried to persuade us. "Look, the factory is full of ammunition and explosives. Whoever stays here will be killed."

The back gate of the factory opened wide. The factory spread over several miles and this exit outside Czenstochow was unknown to us. Broad fields covered with snow two meters high were revealed, and the Germans drove a path for us through the snow. Soon we found ourselves on the road leading to the factory, which was clear of snow because trucks passed there all day long. Along this road we left the Hasag factory.

A few girls who knew we were from Czenstochow approached us. They thought that, as locals, we knew where we were, and would therefore surely escape, and they would simply follow in our footsteps. But we did not know the area, and continued to walk after the Germans, so the other girls left us and escaped on their own. Our cousin and many acquaintances stayed at the factory. There were some who knew of hiding places and helped people to conceal themselves. However, we were five sisters and one brother, and our only concern was to remain together and not to lose any one of our number. Thus, we continued to march after the Germans.

Endless fields of white spread in front of us. Above us stretched clear skies, scattered with stars. Suddenly, the pastoral quiet was shattered. A loud noise was heard and the fields trembled. Bombs began to fall one after the other. We saw them hit the roofs of houses, a great fire rising up after them. They were mostly incendiary bombs.

"Maybe we should stay here among the heaps of snow?" the idea crossed my mind.

"The end of the war is so close you can almost feel it," said my sister.

My sisters and I held each other's hands, with Chanoch between us. We all considered escaping, but we were afraid to actually try it. If the bombing continued for a day or two, we might freeze in the cold. And what if the Germans came to look for us in the morning and killed those who had dropped out?

"There's no choice," we decided unanimously. "We must continue." Most of the girls "dropped out" along the way. At all events, we tried to walk at the end of the line, in order to leave our options open. But it was not long before we found ourselves at the head of the convoy, thanks to the many "deserters" along the way.

Chapter Thirty-four

The Train

We continued to walk all night without stopping. Relatively speaking we were not heavily guarded: only five armed Ukrainians accompanied us. Even so, thoughts of the labor camp gave us no rest and we thought of escape until the very last moment.

Just before dawn we reached a spot some ten miles from Czenstochow. Along the route some Poles told us, "The Russians have occupied Czenstochow!"

How sorry we were that we had not hidden. We could have held out for a few hours, even in those snowy fields. Perhaps even now we could still be saved....

A thin layer of frozen snow crunched lightly beneath our feet. A cold, sharp wind blew in our faces and stabbed our bodies with sharp needles. We were tired and frozen. A temperature of minus 20° C reigned outside. I was wearing knee socks and thin shoes. I felt as if my frozen limbs were rebelling against me. Even my mouth was frozen and I couldn't utter a sound. In the meantime, a German came with a bucket of white paint.

"What's this?" we wondered wordlessly. But we were not left to wonder for very long. He took a brush, dipped it in white paint, and marked a large white cross on our backs. Now we were marked...all was lost. If we tried to escape we would be caught immediately; no one could stay out in this cold without a coat.

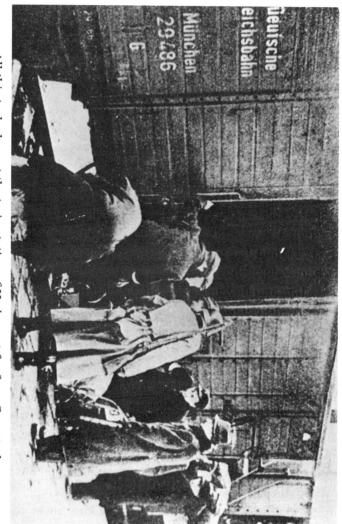

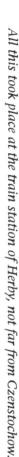

All this took place at the train station of Herby, not far from Czenstochow.

Minutes later, five Germans wearing SS caps separated the men from the women. Of 2000 people who had left Hasag, only 850 reached Herby, the village where we now found ourselves.

"What will happen?" we asked each other. "They're separating the men from the women! They'll take Chanoch from us! Should we dress him as a girl?"

"It's not worth it," other people intervened. "If the Germans find out you've tricked them, it will be terrible."

"Yes. They'll probably carry out a medical examination; after all, they only want healthy people."

Thus we stood in two groups facing each other. Aside from Chanoch, four other children, together with their fathers, were included among the "men." Chanoch looked at us and we gazed back at him without speaking. Our hearts ached at this parting. "Will we meet again?" I wondered silently. "Who knows?" In my desperation, I lifted my eyes to heaven, a single prayer in my heart. "Please God, please help us to come through the war safely and to be reunited...."

Chanoch stood facing us, small and thin, his eyes full of fear and helplessness. In his pockets was the crust of bread we had given him and a tiny pan. How I loved him! I wanted so much to run to him, to stretch out my hands to him and hug him. But no, it was forbidden.... The Germans would kill us both. And just now, at the end of the war! I restrained myself with all my might. Soon, just a little longer, we would be free.

This took place at the train station of Herby, not far from Czenstochow.

The whistle of the train and the clang of its wheels could be heard from afar. When the freight cars drew up alongside us, the command was given in German: "Get going!"

At that moment I recalled many trains, long, long, trains — the ones which had carried the people of Bialystock and others... would we, too, be taken to those same places of dread? But I was so tired and cold that I willingly got onto the train. All I wanted was a place to sit with my sisters beside me. Immediately we sought each other out. Chanoch remained below, among the men. Another look and then another. The Germans had reverted to their usual behavior — coarseness. We were pushed and shoved into the freight car and when it was full, a Ukrainian got in with us, lest we escape....

The Ukrainian settled himself in the carriage, lit a tin of coals, and happily warmed his hands and feet. Later, he took out a tasty sandwich, wrapped in paper, and began to eat with gusto. Again, the engine whistle sounded and the train moved off. One thought troubled all of us: where to?...

The next day, the Ukrainian left the car and locked us in after him. The train continued its journey. In all, we traveled for about ten days. Sometimes the railway lines were filled with German soldiers and we couldn't move. Through the cracks in the walls we watched the German soldiers and noticed that there was much activity. We were hungry and thirsty and the train was sealed; no one entered or left. Every crumb of bread we had brought was long since eaten. Some girls stood near a small opening in the roof of the car and tried to take a little snow to melt in their mouths. We were about one hundred girls in there, and it was an impossible task to reach the opening. However, we could peek out through the cracks in the walls. What a beautiful world I saw there! White fields and forests, with rays of sunshine falling on them and lighting them with additional splendor in all the colors of the rainbow. The rivers and lakes, some of which were covered with ice, were also astounding in their beauty. The strong sunlight sparkled on the slabs of ice and revealed wonderful colors. We passed through towns and villages, and one of the girls, a native of Germany, recognized Berlin, the capital.

How long would we have to stay cooped up in the freight car? Where were the Germans taking us? And what did they plan to do with us when we got there?

Chapter Thirty-five

Ravensbruck

The doors to the freight car were locked with iron bolts which could be opened only from the outside. The frost penetrated the car, and not a few toes and fingers froze. Not everyone had enough room to sit and from time to time we would change places with those who stood.

After standing for a whole day, my strength gave out. Hunger, thirst, and cold clouded my brain, and I felt the floor moving slowly towards the ceiling. I fainted. When I came to, I could not find my legs. Some of the girls were lying on them. Even my hands were lying somewhere under other girls' heads. My own head was pounding fiercely, but I was happy to be able to feel it, unlike my hands and feet.

My sister saw that my condition was serious and gave me a tiny piece of bread which she had left. I held it in my mouth like a candy and this brought me to myself. I aroused myself from my faint and felt I was coming back to life.

There was a worried silence in the crowded car. No one had the strength to speak, and we were all downcast. From time to time one or another of the girls would faint — and there was nothing with which to revive her. Nobody had any food left.

"Master of the Universe, will we travel straight to Heaven in these railway carriages?"

After twelve days, the train stopped at a side station, and

two Germans ordered us, "Get out immediately!"

There was no response.

"You'll get food here!" they added.

These magic words inspired us to try to get to our feet, although even then, not everyone managed. When the Germans saw that the carriage was still not emptied, they got onto the car and began to shower blows left and right with sticks and rifle butts. The unfortunate girls got to their feet, but some of them simply fell back helpless. The Germans then ordered them to be taken off by force.

We trembled with cold, but were given a cup of hot water and two potatoes. It had been a long time since we had tasted such delicacies.

Meanwhile, the carriages were cleaned by some of the stronger girls, who were given extra food in return. Then we were given the order to reboard. This time, we were equipped with two buckets which served as latrines.

A metallic clanging heralded the sealing of the carriages, and the journey continued. We did not know where we were bound, but we realized that we were in Germany. The train traveled for several hours and then stopped again. I pressed my eye to the crack and saw people, heard the sound of the German language, but was none the wiser for it. Day after day the train stood there, and we, imprisoned within. Each day we made a mark on the wall as another day passed. Light shined through the cracks and thus we distinguished between day and night.

With nothing to occupy us, without food, drink, or exercise, we passed those dismal days. We folded our legs under our chins for lack of space, and when we felt we were about to freeze we stood up. A whole week passed before the train rocked and swayed and set off once more. Eight days had passed since our last meal of water and potatoes. Despair spread among us. Did the Germans plan to kill us by starvation? Our last spark of hope had faded. I recalled a well-known German saying: "It's no disaster to lose money, but if you lose the will to live — all is lost!"

Once again, the train stopped somewhere for a day. Then somebody began to fiddle with the locks and the door opened wide. The Germans assumed that some of us were no longer alive, but this didn't bother them at all. With a shout they ordered us out, and immediately, they leapt aboard and began to shower us indiscriminately with blows. Whoever could still stand on her feet, got only a small portion of the blows, but the weaker ones got the "thorough treatment" and were taken off barely alive.

I saw how one German kicked two girls who couldn't rise with his heavy boots; each blow hurt as if it had landed on my own back.

"Get into lines!" barked the Germans, and rows of five girls were formed. The Germans then counted us and ordered, "Forward, march!"

We walked for about twelve miles, until we got to the Ravensbruck camp. As the great iron gates of the notorious women's camp swallowed us up, the Germans went into their house near the camp entrance and enjoyed a large meal, accompanied by singing and music. The sounds of their voices could be heard through the windows — the senseless babble of drunkards.

In the meantime, we had already stood outside for half an hour, exposed to the frightful cold. A few local women — veteran inmates, approached us. "Have you got gold and diamonds? Give them to us!" No one answered. "They'll take it from you anyway!" they explained.

The women were skinny and their heads were shaved so that they hardly looked female at all. In fact, I thought they were men. Their faces were skull-like, bones covered in skin with only their expressionless eyes staring out at us. They wore dirty caps on their heads and their bodies were covered with befouled rags.

We looked at these women. There was no telling their age or origin. Perhaps archeologists might have learned something about them... from their bones.

The door of the house opened and four fat, large women came out, typical specimens of the German lower class.

"Get in lines — five across!" they screamed in chorus.

"First four rows — to the bathhouse!"

Without even giving us time to respond to the order, their clubs began to fly. Fear and terror seized us...we had heard how people were sent into the "showers" and brought out as corpses. Perhaps the locals hadn't had time to tell us of the crematoria?

I whispered a silent prayer to our Father in Heaven: "Please protect us even more closely, now that the war is coming to an end." I heard my sisters praying *"Shema Yisrael"*...perhaps this was our last prayer...I hoped we wouldn't have to suffer long.

The first twenty girls went into the bathhouse and we trembled with cold and fear.

Once again, the veteran prisoners sneaked up to us.

"Is this a death camp?" we asked.

"This is a women's camp," replied the prisoners. "There are 90,000 women here from all over Europe, Jews and Christians."

Wild cries disturbed our conversation; the four Germans ordered us to "get in line" and continued to assail us with their clubs. Again, twenty of us were counted, my sisters and myself among them. Accompanied by blows and kicks in every possible place, we were pushed into the bathhouse.

Chapter Thirty-six

Hela's Illness

The bathhouse was in a small hut not far away. In the ante-room some clerks sat behind writing desks and recorded our personal data. They wanted to know my father's name, family name, age, ethnic origins, religious affiliations, and so on.

"What superb organization!" I thought to myself. "Why do these accursed Germans need our personal details before we die?"

In orderly fashion, five girls, one row at a time, would enter the bathhouse. When my turn came, I answered all the questions, and my replies were recorded in a large register. I got a number beginning with "96" and followed by three digits.

"From now on," the German clerk warned me, "Ruth Dziubas does not exist — only that number!" She pushed into my hand a piece of paper with my new number on it.

"Learn it by heart!" she ordered. "You must be prepared to reply to every call according to that number only!" she added.

After that, we entered the larger room and were examined by German doctors who wanted to make sure that we were fit for work and free of infectious diseases.

Throughout the examinations I stood close to my sister and prayed that we would not be parted. The next step was the wash-room — and it was real! Then on to a third room, where each of us was given a dress, shoes, coat, and head scarf. Our own clothes were not returned to us. "These clothes must be disinfected," they said.

I sadly regretted the loss of the photographs of my dear parents which I had hidden in my shoe, the pictures of my little brothers, and the gold button covered with cloth on my coat. But most of all, I regretted the loss of my miniature prayer book which I had kept in the pocket of my coat, and which I had guarded during every search — or perhaps the contrary was true and it had guarded me...?

Our clothes were piled up in a large heap, and the corpulent Germans, who had apparently once been criminal prisoners, watched to make sure that no one approached the heap. While my hand was still outstretched to receive my parcel of clothes, I saw girls leaving by the rear exit. "I know that girl from somewhere," I thought, and strained my memory to remember. "Who is she? From where do I know her?" The girl sensed my wondering gaze upon her and whispered: "I am your friend, Miriam." Miriam! How she had changed! Only an hour earlier we had stood together outside! Now, a creased black kerchief covered her shaven head and her beautiful figure was draped in a large man's coat, which reached her ankles. The shoulders were very wide and, in the absence of buttons, the coat was tied with string. Underneath, her feet peeped out, shod in huge, slightly crooked, men's shoes. I was shocked by her appearance; would I, too, look like that? And my beautiful sisters?

Most of the girls, especially those with long hair, were shaved immediately. The clothes we received were varied and odd. Tall girls wore short dresses and vice versa. The Germans made very sure that we didn't trade the clothes among ourselves. To my lot fell a silk summer dress. It was dark blue with a large décolleté back and front. At that time, I had grown taller and my neck had lengthened, so that I was nicknamed "long neck." To this "ballgown" were added torn men's shoes, with open uppers; obviously someone had looked for gold or money in them.

When we finished dressing, we were taken outside through another door and from there to our new living quarters. This was a large hut with two huge rooms and three little ones. One small room was used as a washroom, with fifteen sinks and taps, one alongside the other, while the other two were bathrooms.

Three-tiered wooden bunks were arranged in the big rooms from floor to ceiling. Along each row lay women, dreadfully crowded together, each one allotted a space some thirty centimeters wide. Under these conditions one could lie only on one side of one's body.

In this room alone, 1000 women slept each night! The stench and filth were terrible. Each morning a long line of women would form near the sinks to wash their hands and mouths at least once a day. Side by side with the women lived the lice which sucked the little blood they had. The old-timers would pluck them absentmindedly from their bodies, and there were those who had become quite expert at their removal.

After several days at Ravensbruck, my sister Hela fell ill with a bad attack of dysentery. We couldn't even provide her with clean drinking water. Every morning we got about one-half liter of hot, dirty water — perhaps it was dishwater — and one slice of moldy bread. At noon we got stinking water again, this time with the addition of a little starch. Hela got weaker and weaker, and there was no possibility of giving her even minimal aid.

Two days later I, too, was heavily stricken with diarrhea. At night, our sixth night at Ravensbruck, I suddenly felt an urgent need to relieve myself. This was no easy matter. We lay as tidily and tightly packed as sardines in a can, with fifty girls on one side of me and seventy girls on the other. In the dense overcrowding, no one could turn over if her 120 bedfellows did not turn with her. However, my condition was serious, and I was compelled to move.

In the pitch darkness, without seeing where I was going, I climbed over the bodies, my teeth clenched. After much wearisome toil, I reached the end of the row and began to climb down from the second story. Suddenly I felt that I could no longer control myself.

A Czech woman, who had arrived a week earlier and was still in good shape, set up a terrible commotion — swearing and cursing at me so that her screams roused the whole barrack.

"I promise you!" she yelled. "You'll see! I'll catch her! I'll kill her with my own hands! She'll pay for this!"

Shocked and trembling, I fumbled my way until I reached my destination — the bathroom — whose location was not yet quite clear to me. After a long while, I decided to return; perhaps I would manage to rest on my bunk for a while and calm the violent pains in my stomach. I groped along the walls with my hand in the total darkness.

Suddenly I heard more shouts. "Thief, catch her! She stole two slices of bread from me!"

The tiered beds in the concentration camps

Chapter Thirty-seven

"Stop Thief"

Strong hands caught hold of me. The electric light went on and I could not escape. "I'm lost!" I thought. "How can I prove that I *didn't* eat those two slices of bread?"

The block *kapo* (supervisor) pushed me roughly and dug her long nails into my body. She was cruel and capable of strangling girls without blinking an eye; for her, there was no more to it than killing a fly. She took law and order into her own hands, and she ruled our barracks absolutely. We were all terrified of her.

"I'll teach you, and all the rest, to steal in my hut!" she yelled. Her bulging eyes terrorized me. Again, I turned to the Creator. "Please God, save me from these strangling hands. Only You can save me now God...." Then, in the midst of my shock and fear an idea occurred to me. "I'll show her my soiled clothes! Perhaps then she'll believe that I am not at all capable of eating anything."

An angel from Heaven must certainly have helped me convince the *kapo* to listen to me. She let go of my hand and released my neck from her nails. I fled....

Those same stains on my clothes which had caused me such grief had saved me. I saw clearly that one must always say, "This, too, is for the best," with the real belief that everything comes from Heaven. Our Father above has shown me great kindness and saved me.

However, my nocturnal adventures did not end there. When I drew near to our room I heard the Czech gentile still busy with her curses and imprecations, announcing that she was waiting for "that girl." I was frightened to go back to my sister, lest the Czech catch me and finish me off with her strong muscular arms. I waited. To my good fortune, the lights soon went on in our room and the order to rise was given.

Within half an hour, 2,000 women had to leave the barrack for roll call. The ones who arrived last always got severe blows, but just going through the opening of the door took time.

I saw my sisters getting down from the bunk and waited for them. Together we went out to roll call. We did not have to get dressed in the morning, it was not at all customary to change one's clothes in the camp... we didn't even remove our shoes. No one separated from whatever possessions she had, even for a moment. Fortunately, the Czech did not recognize me. Apparently, she suspected someone else.

The roll call at Ravensbruck was an especially difficult experience. We stood outside, in a temperature of minus 20° C, our hands raised, for two hours, from 5:00 to 7:00 A.M. We had to arrange ourselves in lines of ten, and each row had to be absolutely straight. Between the rows was a space of half a meter so that the Germans could inspect our order. They would pass between the rows to check if all hands were raised. If one of us lowered them, even for a split second, she was immediately punished, and her neighbors too were given "treatment."

It was still dark outside and our arms ached dreadfully. God in Heaven, do You see us? After all, we are Your chosen people....

In those moments I would remember how Mother would tell us of the suffering of the Jews in Egypt. As she talked she would sigh and wipe her eyes.

For us, the stories of the Jews in Egypt were not merely stories; we ourselves suffered them on our flesh, each moment.

*   *   *

One morning I stood next to my friend Miriam. I glanced at her out of the corner of my eye. She looked sickly and weak. "What happened to you Miriam?" I whispered in Polish.

"I have had diarrhea for three days," she whispered back. "I haven't eaten at all. But it doesn't matter — I'm rich now."

"What do you mean?"

"I am a woman of property! Three slices of bread! I've already planned what I'll buy with them."

"What?"

"I'll tell you. With one slice I shall buy whole shoes!"

"And with the second?"

"For the second I want a warm coat."

"And the third?"

"The third slice will get me a warm head scarf for my head," she smiled.

"How did you manage to hoard such a treasure?" I wondered.

"I'll show you." Miriam decided to take the risk. She lowered one hand to show me the bag on her shoulder where she kept her treasure.

Then she gasped aloud. "My bag! My bag! It's gone!"

From her shoulder dangled a lone piece of string, the only remnant of the hoard which it had held. Miriam's heart was broken. For three days she had not eaten, and only the thought of the warm clothes she would buy had kept her going. Now, her dream was shattered. I saw that weakness was overcoming her and she could barely stand on her feet. I wanted to hold her, but I was afraid that we would both pay for that gesture with our lives. The German walked up and down with a submachine gun in his hand. Woe to the one whom that gun touched.

I forgot my own problems and whispered words of encouragement to my friend.

"Catch hold of yourself, Miriam. Hang on! Watch out, the German is coming." He passed us and did not stop. I felt with all my heart that, in spite of everything, a watchful eye was being kept on us from above.

"See. God helps us and He will help you even with torn shoes. We haven't much more time to serve here. Just remember that."

That day, I was sent to gather wood, not far from the camp. In one of the abandoned huts, I saw, to my terror, a woman lying lifeless on the floor. She had frozen to death. It was the first time that I had seen a dead body from up close, and the scene haunted me for many days and nights.

"Who was that woman? How did she get to the hut? Was she Jewish? Perhaps she hid in the hut and met her death there?" The questions pierced my mind.

I did not share the experience with anyone else. I felt it was superfluous; we saw enough tragic sights as it was.

Chapter Thirty-eight

Parting from Hela

After we had been at Ravensbruck for about two weeks, the Germans decided to transfer our group to a labor camp. At this time, the Russians were approaching Auschwitz, and most of those prisoners who were not murdered or driven on the notorious death marches were transferred to camps in Germany, and among them to Ravensbruck.

It was mid-February, 1945. The cold was unbearable, about minus 25° C. We wrapped our torn shoes in rags, but these soon became wet and then turned to ice. Their weight made walking difficult; we could hardly drag our feet along. In addition, our stomachs were empty, and we were plagued by pangs of hunger. Meanwhile, the rumor spread that some women were to be moved to another camp.

"We won't object to being sent away," we concluded.

"It is not likely that anywhere could be worse than this," added my sister.

But the question arose from the depths of our hearts, "What about Hela?"

This was a truly bitter problem. Hela suffered constantly from dysentery and was so weak, she could scarcely walk. In our two weeks at Ravensbruck she had become barely a shadow of her former self and was hardly recognizable. She had been so beautiful and so young — only in her twenties. We didn't want to let her go to the hospital because the Germans used to go there every few days and liquidate anyone who could not stand on her feet.

Each one of us sisters had a gold ring which we wore beneath a small bandage on our fingers. Miraculously, in spite of all the searches, they had remained in our possession. "Perhaps we'll sell the rings in exchange for a travel permit for Hela," we thought to ourselves.

We went to consult with some of the local Jewish women who had been around for some months and were experts in "ways and means."

"In our opinion," said the women, "the journey you face won't be any easier than the one you have already suffered; without food, without water, without any provisions for the road...do you see your sister surviving under such conditions?"

One of the women added: "The journey may take as long as three weeks."

We looked at each other; it was clear to us that Hela could not withstand such a journey.

"Perhaps we sisters could all hide ourselves in the camp until after the transport has left?"

"Impossible," warned the old-timers. "This is not Hasag...if you don't get your daily bread ration, you'll not find other food. It means certain death by starvation."

Although Hela tried to relieve our sadness, we were brokenhearted at the prospect of separation.

"You must leave me and go," she said. "God will help us, and perhaps we will soon meet again."

"How can we leave you here, Hela?" we asked anxiously.

"I don't know if I could survive the journey. I feel drained of strength. I'm just not up to traveling — I probably couldn't even get myself onto the train. Please go, and God will help you and save you," she added.

I cried bitterly all night. My tears wet my coat. Doubts tortured my mind. Must we part? This parting might be forever....

"Master of the World, protect Hela!" I prayed. "Help her in her desperate need!"

I must have fallen asleep, because the ringing of the bell suddenly reached my ears, along with the shouts of the *kapo*: "Get up!"

She repeated her deafening shout. Roll call was in half an hour. I leapt from my perch on the third level and hurried to the washroom. Perhaps for once I would manage to wash my hands and face.

This time I succeeded. Five or ten minutes later, I saw how the others were driven out of the barrack with clubs.

It was still dark outside. The roofs of the huts and the trees outside the fence were covered with snow. All around us the world still slept... only we, the inmates of Ravensbruck, were already standing in the big yard. For us, the night's rest had ended.

We hurried to arrange ourselves in rows before the blows fell. The order was given: "Hands up!" and several thousand hands were raised.

After one hour we were notified over the loudspeaker: "Attention! If your number is called, go immediately to the right, beside the barracks!"

The numbers floated out into the air, and I suddenly heard mine: 96,253. Yes, that was it.

I lowered my hands and marched to the right. "I hope my sisters come, too," I prayed in my heart. My prayer was answered. When I reached the place, my three sisters were already there. Hela was not among them.

Actually, almost all the girls from the Hasag transport were there, together with a few other women who had not yet become *musselmen.*

Our group received an order to form rows and were then counted. Finally, the iron gate opened and we departed.

Some of the camp inmates stood by and watched us jealously from a distance, as if we had suddenly been granted a hap-

pier fate than theirs. They believed we were being moved to a labor camp in which we would be given more food and would thus
be enabled to survive the war.

We looked back, and our hearts contracted. Among the
women, I recognized Hela. It seemed that she wanted to let us
know that she was all right, that we shouldn't worry about her —
after all, she could walk....

Hela, so refined and beautiful...how she had aged in those
last weeks. She must have felt my gaze on her, for a little smile
alighted on her face, and once again she appeared to me the same
beautiful Hela.

Again and again I whispered a prayer to God to help her to
hold out, not to give way....

Chapter Thirty-nine

Journey into the Unknown

At the head and the rear of the convoy, as well as on both sides, marched Germans, to prevent any escape. We walked thus for about two hours, until we reached the railway station. On a side track stood two cattle wagons.

"Get on!" came the order loudly, immediately accompanied by blows from rifle butts to our heads and faces. We were herded like frightened cows into the wagons. I repeated my prayer that I just not be separated from my sisters, my source of strength.

When the Germans were finally convinced that it was impossible to squeeze in any more girls, they threw in two empty buckets and bolted the wagon from the outside.

They then repeated the procedure with the remaining girls, who were packed into the second wagon. Their harsh German voices and the thud of blows pained our ears.

At the sound of the whistle, the train moved off. We stood packed together so tightly that even when the train rocked, we didn't need to hang on to anything in order not to fall over; there simply wasn't room....

For the first few hours we stood in complete silence. From time to time, one of the girls would call out the name of a friend or relative, in order to ascertain her presence. To my joy, I recognized my sisters standing near me, and my heart filled with gratitude to God.

After a few hours' journey, the train stopped and we passed an entire day in the stationary wagon, standing on our feet the entire time. We began to realize that our journey would be a long one, at least several days — perhaps even several weeks. I looked for a tiny space where perhaps I could sit down, but without success. After standing throughout the day, I fainted. I was not the only one to collapse from lack of food and air. I awoke, and gathered the various parts of my body. After this, I was given space to sit on the floor of the wagon. Slowly, slowly, I filled my lungs with air and recovered a bit.

The journey went on and on. We were given no food, and no one checked up on us; it was as if we were completely forgotten.

Sometimes the train stopped and we would hear the air-raid warning and echoes of bombing. The Germans hid underneath the train, but we were left imprisoned with no means of escape should a bomb hit. Fears assailed me — perhaps the war would end and we would be left here, abandoned, closed into these cattle cars, unable to give any sign of life? Perhaps the Allied soldiers would think that these were empty cattle wagons and wouldn't bother to check them?

At last, after a journey of eleven days, the train stopped, and this time we heard the scrape and rattle of the locks: "Out!"

At first, none of us were capable of getting up. Then we gathered strength, fueled by the hope of receiving a slice of bread and water. I murmured a prayer to the Almighty: "Please let me get up, just to walk a few steps...." I thought constantly of the war and refused, now, to accept the idea of surrender. I made it. I got to my feet, helping another girl as I did so. My sisters limped at my side. Many of the girls were tottering on frostbitten toes. Most of us had lost all feeling in our fingers.

Unfortunately, out of 150 girls, fifty could not get up under any circumstances. In compliance with the orders, we arranged ourselves in rows outside. We looked like paper soldiers that any

wind could blow over and sweep away. Baskets full of bread stood
near the train, and a German distributed a piece to each girl, together with a little water. Those girls who appeared to be in somewhat better shape were ordered to clean the wagons. They took
out the buckets and emptied them, and were then ordered to
"clean" the wagons of the girls who lay there unconscious.

*   *   *

The clear light of day blinded our eyes after the dark, sealed
wagon. A cold sun looked indifferently down upon us; the snow
still covered the surroundings, and it was very cold. I looked at
the beautiful landscape, the little houses where, presumably, German peasants lived. How good it must be to live in a house, with
a family....

"Run!" We were shocked by the order. But knowing that we
had no choice, we tried to run with the last vestiges of our
strength. The sight of the limping, faltering girls amused the Germans. Whoever did not manage to run was beaten until she fell
in the snow — and stayed there....

The next order was: "Get on the train!" and whoever was
able to do so, obeyed. The others remained outside and were
transferred to another wagon, which was somewhat broken.

In a corner of the wagon was a small aperture, and a few of
the girls pressed close to it so that they could ascertain where we
were.

"There are other trains here also," they reported.

"Let us see. What kind of trains?"

"Trains with human passengers — their carriages are closed,
too."

The stronger girls who were able to climb up to the aperture
had an additional advantage; they managed from time to time to
catch a little bit of the snow which fell ceaselessly. Neither I nor
my sisters could manage this.

Once again, I sat in the same position, my legs folded under
my chin. The bitter cold penetrated the very fibers of my body,

reaching inwards. It was as if that single slice of bread had never entered my stomach. Hunger and thirst shriveled my heart and twisted my insides. My empty intestines were sewn up without string and composed their own symphony of hunger.

"I'm happy," I said to myself, "that our sister Hela is not here with us. She wouldn't have survived. Perhaps in Ravensbruck, God will help her."

Once again, we traveled in silence. From time to time, the train stopped in some out-of-the-way place for a few days. After ten days the carriages were opened and, once again, we were ordered out of our prison.

This time, only a few girls were capable of responding. The Germans therefore ordered the first three "passengers" to throw the others out....

"We'll come in a few minutes to see if the wagons are clean!" they threatened.

My sisters' hands and some of their toes were frostbitten, and they could not rise. With great difficulty, we helped each other to our feet and dragged the weaker ones to the door. From afar, I noticed two Germans coming, as they had threatened, to check the situation.

Suddenly I felt that my fear was giving me the driving force to gather the remnants of my strength and get down from the carriage.

Chapter Forty
Burgau Camp

On the platform, each one of us was given two potatoes and some water to drink. This time they drove us less harshly than before. I assumed that this was for two reasons: First, the presence of the German civilian population, before whom they were reluctant to demonstrate their murderous behavior. The second reason was that they realized that they would have to gather our bodies themselves. Our labor, in our present condition, was unavailable to them.

After another five days on the train, we reached a village called Burgau. When the wagons were opened, we heard that we had reached a labor camp.

"You'll work here and be given food," said the Germans.

Burgau was smaller than Ravensbruck, and the atmosphere was more relaxed. Here, too, we went through the process of bathing, an examination, and receiving a change of clothes, and we were even given new numbers. Each of us was required to wear her number on her wrist and to remember that it was now her name.

In this camp, some of the women prisoners worked in the kitchen. Here we were given a daily ration of potato soup, which seemed to us like a delicacy. We had not tasted hot, cooked food for seven weeks, with the exception of the dirty water at Ravensbruck. Although not everybody managed to get a potato, the soup was clear and salty.

About 200 women, who looked like men, were confined in the camp. Most of them had shaven heads, usually covered with some sort of covering. Here, too, the women wore odd garments — "*alte zachen*" (rags and pickings).

Only 40 percent of the girls who had left Ravensbruck with our transport managed to reach Burgau. We were give nonproductive work — moving stones from place to place. A small group of stronger girls were sent to work in an aircraft factory. They were better fed than we, since the Germans needed them.

My sister Rivka had the task of distributing bread and soup in our hut, and she tried to give everyone a fair and equal ration. Sometimes the soup was thick and sometimes watery, and this became the chief topic of our conversation. More than once, we came to the conclusion that what was needed was a diver who would dive in and fish out a piece of potato.

My sister Bela worked in the kitchen. After a couple of days, Rivka was given a clerical job, in the office of the camp commandant. She knew German well and was an expert typist.

Our third sister Lola was unable to walk and was sent to the hospital. Bela would sneak a piece of her bread ration in to Lola. She did not forget me, either. Neither did Rivka, who got extra rations for working in the office.

The hospital consisted of half a hut, in which bunks had been installed. The German doctor notified my sister Lola that her toes were completely frostbitten and would have to be amputated. We were shocked by this decision. We got the impression that this doctor had learned his trade on his patients as he went along.

"Please don't amputate," we begged. "Let her rest, at least for a few days!"

"Nobody asked for your opinion!" he screamed in reply. "I am the boss here and I decide!"

My heart ached. How sad that now, at the very end of the

war, my sister would become a cripple. How would she walk without toes? I prayed once more and asked the Almighty: "Please, make a miracle and don't let them amputate. Let her get well soon."

And indeed, the impossible happened. From the depths of my heart, God heard my prayer, and on the very day the operation was to take place, the doctor fell ill with typhus.

*   *   *

It was now the middle of March, 1945. The skies were clear and the sun shone. The snow melted and the world sparkled.

"Merciful One, help us to hold out!" I prayed over and over again.

When we had been at Burgau for about three weeks, the Germans again called out numbers during the morning roll call. Once again, most of our group was included, and my sisters and I were "sent to the right." We were seized by panic. No one told us why we had been singled out. "Hands up! March!" We all walked out of the gate. Were they going to shoot us now?

We walked along until we came upon a railway line with all-too-familiar wagons. I was relieved. They wouldn't bother transporting us if they were planning to kill us.

The Germans explained: "You are going to another labor camp; they need you there."

"Perhaps it will be better there?" Stubborn hope crept into my heart. I did not dare give expression to this optimism. Everyone around me was downcast, despairing, utterly worn out.

We boarded the wagons, and this time the overcrowding was not serious. We even got "provisions" for the journey — a slice of bread. A cold sweat bathed my body when I recalled our previous travels. Soon the wagons would be closed and the nightmare would repeat itself.

The journey continued. We marked off each day and night to keep track of passing time. We counted one week. No living soul looked in on us. The train traveled and stopped, and we were overcome with despair. "These Germans have decided to starve us to death. That way they'll save money, ammunition, and effort," sighed the girls.

The familiar and detested experience of the silent, terrible journey was repeated. Many of the girls were certain that we would end our days like this, but I, with illogical and unquenchable optimism, never ceased believing that God would hear our prayers and save us.

"But soon, soon," I begged in my heart. "Before it is too late."

Physically, I felt my strength leave me, but my spirit was unbroken. I remembered all the while the passage from Psalms: "The dead do not praise God." I felt that I had to go on living. Even when I fainted, I did not give in and never ceased to fight.

Chapter Forty-one

Turkheim Camp

On the eleventh day of our journey, we heard a creaking outside. We pricked up our ears and, indeed, the wagons were being opened.

"Get out!" commanded the Germans.

We blinked our eyes in the light. But our legs refused to obey us.

The Germans hastened to rain cruel blows upon us, and many fell beneath their clubs. The others got up. Wobbling on my feet, I too managed to stagger off the train. Slowly, slowly, I straightened my legs — and was relieved to see that my sisters were also rising. Strength from above flowed into me, and I even managed to help some of the others. But, once again, about 35 percent of the passengers were unable to move.

When we were arranged in rows of five, the Germans counted us, and some Ukrainians in Gestapo uniform with skulls on their caps lead us for about three-quarters of a mile to the Turkheim camp. The village of Turkheim is about fifteen miles from Mindelheim. This camp for women prisoners was spread over an area of about a mile. An electrified, barbed-wire fence surrounded the camp, and in each of its four corners stood a watchtower, from which we were guarded day and night.

Sometimes, when murderous Nazis or their henchmen got bored, they would practice "target shooting" at any prisoner who approached the fence. This game amused them greatly.

The huts in the camp were built into the ground, so that only the roofs were visible. Each hut consisted of one long room with two benches running along its length. Each bench was about four feet wide.

Between the benches was a space of about twenty-four inches. These benches were our "beds" — about eighteen inches of width per person. Thin, grey blankets were also included in the "deal," as were the white spots which marked them: lice eggs.

We lay down on the benches and stretched our legs. "Thank God for this chance to lie down and rest," I said. I was so exhausted and aching that I hardly felt my body. Even these filthy boards seemed to me like a bed.

The next day, after roll call, I discovered something important: there was water in the washroom! Clean water that could be drunk until all thirst was quenched! I drank and drank, as if I could make up for all the water I had been deprived of during eleven days of thirst. The water flowed into my parched, dried up body and refreshed me.

The ordeal of standing for two hours with raised hands was not spared us. There was only one important difference. After the roll call we were sent to work. For the first days of my stay at Turkheim I was sent with a group of about twenty-five girls to the forest to gather wood. We were accompanied by a heavy guard, lest we escape, Heaven forbid.

It was now April, 1945. How good it was to smell the trees. I worked as hard as I could; I wanted to be sent to the same job again the next day. Here, in the heart of nature, I felt the warm rays of spring.

The snows melted and water flowed from the hills, sweeping away the remnants of snow and ice. Tender green plants began to peep cautiously through the soil, and buds sprang up on the bare branches of the trees.

The world began to awaken from its long winter sleep, and

the sun even smiled on me. Lovely and beautiful, the glory of the world! I tried to mentally photograph what I saw, and store it deep within, where no one could take it away.

Full of hope, I quietly sang a little song of thanks to God, who had protected us from Heaven and who did not forget us even in this valley of death.

After work, we were given a slice of bread and a cup of potato soup. The portions were small, but I counted backwards now. Every day that passed brought us closer to a better tomorrow.

*　　*　　*

One day, when I returned from work and stood in line to get my soup, an argument broke out among the inmates.

"That's my place!" one of the girls shouted, pushing another out of the way.

"What do you mean? It's my place! I won't give way to you!" stormed the other.

"Fighting!?" the German in charge of "order" asked. "Very well! Stop serving soup at once!"

I was among the girls who did not get a portion that day, and I felt very sorry for myself. My stomach contracted and ached with hunger, and my disappointment was acute. I had really looked forward to that meager portion at the end of the day.

Wet, cold, and sad, I stood with my cup in my hand. All I wanted was a bit of hot, salty water. The fresh air in the forest had sharpened my appetite. Lightheaded, I went to the hut and, as I entered, burst into tears.

"Rutka! You're crying?" said my shocked sisters. "What happened to you?"

I was embarrassed to answer, but my disappointment got the better of me: "Two girls had a fight in the lineup and the German stopped giving out soup. I didn't get any!"

Immediately, spontaneously, each one of my sisters handed me the cup in her hand. I was very moved. My sisters were surely just as hungry as I was myself, yet they had not hesitated to share their own small portions with me. Very few people would have been capable of such an act in those hard times.

*   *   *

Night fell and the lights went out.

I lay on the bench and tucked the grey blanket, which was too short and too thin, around my battered body. My misery and sheer tiredness made me unable to fall asleep. I tossed and turned uncomfortably. The lice had been waiting all day for their nightly feast and now began to energetically suck our blood.

"Whew," I fumed. "These lice!"

No doubt I managed to kill a considerable number of them, but even more continued to feast when I, "battle-weary," eventually fell asleep.

Chapter Forty-two

The Escape

April 20, 1945. The village of Turkheim was being bombed. We saw planes passing over our heads and bombs falling, followed by earsplitting explosions. Everyone threw themselves flat on the ground to avoid the splinters. Screams and prayers were heard everywhere. The Jews among us cried out *"Shema Yisrael."*

"Lord of the Universe! Save us! Don't let us be killed now!" These bombings were aimed at the Germans themselves, and I believed with all my heart that these would be our last hours of suffering. All we had to do was stay alive.

With renewed hope, I joyfully greeted each Allied bomb as a harbinger of salvation. However, I kept these thoughts to myself. Then I did a strange thing; I began to review my Latin grammar, with all the pronouns and verbs. I would have to remember what I had learned earlier in order to continue studying after the war.

The Latin grammar gave way to other thoughts: Where were all our near and dear ones? My father, my brothers Mendel and Chanoch? And how was Hela faring in Ravensbruck? Most people at the camp responded differently than I did. They were full of fear that right now, after so much suffering, the Germans would suddenly choose to kill us.

The next morning, nobody went to work. The bombing continued, more heavily than before. Most of the Germans left the camp and only a few remained. The outside guard posts continued to be manned, as usual, by the Ukrainians.

Someone came up with the brilliant idea, "Let's go to the food store!" but disappointment awaited us there. The shelves were bare. The Germans had left only onions and potatoes.

Utter chaos reigned in the camp. Some of the male prisoners now arrived from their compound and took all the food that came to hand. They broke the wooden benches and tore them to shreds in order to set fire to them. It seemed that German rule was at an end.

Many of the prisoners did not take part in the festivities. They could not even stand on their feet. These lay silently on their "beds" and stared vacantly into space. Whoever could still muster an ounce of strength filled his belly with potatoes.

One of the men succeeded in lighting a fire under the huge pot in which the soup was cooked. He filled it with water, put each one of his potatoes into his stockings, and lowered it into the water to boil.

My sisters and some girls with whom we had become friendly said, "We should store these potatoes as provisions for the journey."

Unanimously we had decided that at the first opportunity we would escape.

"We won't repeat the mistake we made at Czenstochow."

The next day the bombing stopped, and some Germans appeared and informed us, "The bombing is not over yet! We want to save you, and we will transfer you to another camp!"

Behind the scenes we had been told that the "rescue camp" referred to was the infamous Dachau, near Munich, the capital of Bavaria. This concentration camp had become notorious as early as 1936, when Germans who opposed Hitler were sent there.

No! We would not be tricked again. We would exploit any and every opportunity, every slackness on the part of the Germans.

Meanwhile, the Germans ordered us to form lines. "It's

quite a long way to the railway, about two and a half miles," they said with pretended kindness.

This time, too, we were accompanied by an armed German guard, but we could sense the slackening of discipline. Along the way, a bomb whistled over us. Everyone, including the Germans, fell flat on the ground. As we lay there, we planned our escape.

"Now!" we decided, "with no further delay!"

There was a few minutes' break in the bombing, and we all got to our feet and continued to walk. In the distance, a forest sparkled green before us. We decided: "That's the place!" As we advanced, one after the other the girls drew closer to the forest. The Germans also saw the advantages of the forest. "By going this way, it will be easier to hide from the bombs," they said.

The Germans did not imagine that any of us would think of escaping. We exchanged hints among ourselves in Polish so as not to arouse their suspicions. There were ten of us involved, we four sisters and six friends from the camp.

"At the next bombing, each one escapes to the forest! We'll meet a few hundred feet inside." We had the advantage that the Germans lost their heads during the bombing.

"We mustn't wait until they get used to the noise of the explosions," we whispered to each other. After an hour of marching, the bombing began again. We gathered strength, took our courage in both hands, and fled into the forest. The Germans shot at us, but without their usual enthusiasm — no prizes awaited them now for murdering young girls.

My sister Lola could walk only with great difficulty, due to her frostbitten toes. She weighed only sixty pounds — all skin and bones, and her legs looked like matchsticks.

We had almost reached the forest when Rivka suddenly stopped in her tracks.

"Lola is missing!" she said, panic stricken. "I'm going back!"

"I'll come with you!" I said, and we both went back to look for her.

"Here she is!" a cry of joy burst from our lips.

We ran towards her and caught hold of her. Bullets passed over our heads as the Germans sighted and shot at us, but Heaven helped us and we came through unharmed.

In the depths of the forest, the other girls already awaited us. We stood and breathed in the sweet air. For the first time in ages, we were happy.

Chapter Forty-three

In the Forest

April 24, 1945. Probably Pesach time, our Festival of Freedom. I thought of the Exodus of the Jews from Egypt. Here, now, the miracles which God had wrought for our Fathers and for us were being clearly unrolled before our eyes: "With a strong hand and an outstretched arm — from slavery to freedom...."

Meanwhile, the road to freedom was a long one. Many dangers lay in wait for us in the forest. However, in comparison to the concentration camps of the accursed Germans, we felt ourselves to be in an earthly paradise. In a small clearing, we prepared a spacious sleeping area for ourselves and all the other girls. We lay down on the blankets we had brought with us when we had prepared our provisions at the start of our journey. We breathed in deeply the air of freedom and basked in the giddy feeling of liberty, with no guns, no clubs, far from the shouts of the Germans and the loathsome sight of the SS hats with the death's head symbol on them. Now we were close to the Almighty and He protected us.

"Dear God," I prayed, "avenge our brothers and all the House of Israel who went to their deaths for the sanctification of Your Name." I thought of my mother and brother, for whom I had long since given up hope; the bitter truth was very clear to me.

*   *   *

A pastoral peace reigned all about us. It seemed to me that I was at the height of some lovely dream. I sat up and hummed to myself a wonderful melody by Strauss about the Vienna woods. It exactly suited my mood at that moment.

Stripes of red and yellow showed through the undergrowth and between the trees. The setting sun seemed to be sending us former prisoners a good-night blessing. We curled up close to one another and whispered the prayer *Shema Yisrael* from the depths of our hearts. I added an additional heartfelt prayer of thanks to God for all His kindness.

Then, quite unbidden, other thoughts crept into my mind. Where would we go from here? How would the news of the end of the war get to us? "Never mind," I told myself. "Now we are free! That's the main thing." Fatigue threatened to overwhelm me, but I, savoring every moment of liberty, was reluctant to waste any in sleep.

The song of the birds woke us the next morning. Patches of blue merged with the green of trees, and the sun already stood high in the sky. I was so happy that I began to dance and sing. My friends looked at me doubtfully; a long way still stretched before us — long and fraught with dangers.

After a short morning prayer, we decided to eat the few half-cooked potatoes that we still had with us. We sat down comfortably and breathed in the scent of spring. A little butterfly with white wings frolicked in the fresh air. How I wished we, too, could float along as he did — perhaps even as far as Eretz Yisrael....

Suddenly, one of the girls straightened up and said, "Quiet! Someone's coming!"

Before our horrified eyes, there appeared a pair of shiny black boots — a Nazi uniform — and behind him three more.

The smile of happiness froze on my lips, and the blood seemed to freeze in my veins. The girls were silent, as if overtaken by thunder on a clear day.

"Lord of the Universe!" I pleaded in my heart, "You have brought us so far, don't leave us now! Only yesterday did we cast off our fetters and taste liberty."

No one moved. We sat as if nailed to the spot, and screamed silently. Then a cry of fear and suffering escaped audibly from the lips of one of the girls.

The officer among the soldiers approached us and went up to my sister Rivka.

"Who are you?" he asked in German. "Where have you come from? What are you doing here?"

Rivka paled and the words stuck in her throat. The soldier looked at the others who sat trembling, in utter despair. A smile passed his lips, and he began to speak in Russian.

"Don't worry," he reassured us. "We are partisans, not Germans. We live in the forest and are trying to get to the Russian front, about twenty-five miles from here."

Following our gaze, he added, "The uniforms help when we make a sortie into a village now and then to get food."

Suddenly, like mushrooms after rain, dozens of soldiers in German uniforms appeared all over the place. They enjoined us to join in their struggle and to aid their war against the accursed Nazis.

Rivka took courage and said to the officer, "Sir, please understand our position. We are weak and exhausted; we escaped from the concentration camp only yesterday, and we have no strength to walk any further. Let us stay here.... We love the Russians, but we won't object to being liberated by the Americans if they get here first."

The officer, who listened attentively to Rivka, turned to his soldiers and said, "Let them be. Don't make them join us against their will."

He turned and looked at us again, bowed towards Rivka, and left us.

"Gather up the equipment," he ordered his soldiers. "Forward march! No time to waste!" Unwillingly, the soldiers obeyed and left.

For hours afterwards, the incident troubled us like a nightmare. It was a miracle. I thought that the officer was certainly an angel in disguise. The merits of our righteous forefathers had surely protected us.... Stirred to the depths my being, I again murmured a prayer of thanks to the Almighty, who had, once again, saved us from harm.

We continued to sit on the ground, trembling and frightened. Would there be any more visitors of this kind? Our sense of peace and security was completely shattered. At last, one of the girls got up and began to distribute potatoes among us. The remaining water in the flask was also shared, and we got ready for our second night in the forest.

We spread some of the blankets on the ground and used the others to cover ourselves. I whispered *Shema Yisrael* and cuddled up to my sister Rivka, to draw comfort from her nearness. And so, encouraged by her warmth, I fell asleep.

Chapter Forty-four

Liberation

I awoke and sat up, hugging my knees. "In a single day," I thought to myself wonderingly, "a real change has taken place in nature. It's as if everything, including me, has awoken to life."

The tiny leaves which sprung from the buds had grown in a single day, and their color grew greener and stronger. The rays of sunshine teased them and lit them with a wealth of colors. The eyes blinked at the dazzling display of light and color. Birds flew happily from the branches and looked for twigs and grass to build their nests and start families. Presumably, they had just returned from distant lands; whole flocks of them flew above us in merry song, happy to be back home. Would I, too, be able to return soon to my home? Would I, too, be free to fly like them to my own land? My own homeland?

Indeed, what did it matter, the hunger which gnawed within me, the parching thirst, when matched against the smell of pine. How wonderful to be alive and see the works of Your hand, Lord of the Universe!

But the body, too, has its needs — we had nothing with which to satisfy them. We decided to venture into the town of Turkheim in pairs and look for food.

We decided upon one cover story for us all: "We have been working for peasants and have run away because of the bombing."

Rivka and I went up to a little house on the edge of the forest. We knocked timidly on the door and a German of about
fifty-five years old received us. He didn't seem particularly curi-
ous about us.

"Come into the kitchen," he invited us politely. We followed him and heard him tell his wife, "Give them a good meal."

When we had finished eating, he said, "You can sleep here
tonight." All at once, a loud shout from the front gate mingled
with his words.

"Where are they?" roared a Nazi outside. "I'll kill them! I
won't leave a trace of them!"

Rivka and I looked at each other in bewilderment. We didn't
realize yet that he meant us, but his wild cries frightened us. Our
German host did guess this, and he indicated to his wife that she
smuggle us out the back entrance to the stable. Then he himself
went out to receive his noisy guest.

We crowded into the stable, which housed the German's
three horses. Some pigs who had burst through the fence of their
sty strutted about us, obviously feeling not the least bit uncom-
fortable. We squeezed up against the wall. We weren't at all used
to dealing with domestic animals. The harsh voice of the Nazi
could still be heard cursing and threatening our lives, which, it
turned out, were what he was after. The sound of his heavy steps
reached us as he climbed the stairs of the house to the bedrooms
above. Through a crack in the door, I saw the distinctive boots
worn by the Nazis. A pistol gleamed in his hand, ready for action....

My teeth chattered with terror, and my heart missed more
than one beat. One horse lashed at me with its hairy tail and the
other flopped down on the straw beside me. The pigs snorted as
they wandered back to their sty, affecting great wisdom as they
passed by, their short tails waving to and fro. Were we doomed to
die here in this filthy stable, among the horses and the pigs?

It was getting dark. In every home it was time to sleep. All was silent. Suddenly, I felt as if someone had driven a knife into my heart and it had ceased beating. Tired and weary, I sat down on a pile of hay. I probably lost consciousness for a few seconds. I remember how I opened my eyes and then shut them again, sinking into a deep sleep.

*   *   *

When the first rays of sunshine peeped into the stable, the horses were still lying down. Rivka, who had been sleeping in another corner, awoke first and came over to me. Outside, it was quiet. Then the pigs awoke and raised a racket, demanding to be fed. The German farmer came down and invited us to breakfast in the kitchen.

"You owe me your lives," he stressed. "That Nazi was determined to finish you off before sunrise. He looked all over our house, in all the rooms! You are lucky girls that my wife took the hint and hid you in the stable. That smart fellow didn't dream of looking for you there..." and he chuckled with pleasure when he recalled the angry drunk, wildly searching for us.

I didn't laugh. The fear was still alive within me.

The German looked at his watch. "Quiet!" he said. "It's 11:00 A.M." He turned the knob of the radio to get the latest news.

My sister and I meanwhile surveyed the kitchen, which seemed to us to be the height of luxury. There is nothing like a spacious kitchen, a table with four chairs around it — and above all a radio set, the likes of which we had not seen for six years.

It was April 27, 1945. In dramatic tones, the German newsreader announced: "The Americans have captured the village of Turkheim!"

Turkheim! The very place where we were sitting that minute! The German paled — he understood that the hour of retribution had come. We, on the other hand, burst out in a cry of joy; we were free!

Quickly, I caught Rivka's hand and pulled her after me to the main street. "Come on, let's welcome our saviors!" Outside, we watched in pleasure as the panic-stricken Germans hastily shuttered their windows and bolted their doors.

The fugitives now began to come out. My two other sisters were there, as well as the girls from whom we had separated yesterday and many others from the camp who had not gone on the transport to Dachau, hiding in Turkheim instead.

Freedom! Liberty! The Nazi monster was destroyed! Crushed to death! Choked!!! Along the main street rode American tanks and in them, American soldiers, who replied to our cries of joy by handing out preserves, chocolate, and soap.

Words cannot describe the feeling of happiness that we experienced that day — joy, gladness, happiness, delight; the very words themselves sprang to life once more, danced towards us, bowed, and sang a song of thanks to God. Only a slave, who had subjugated body, heart, and mind to a cruel master, could understand our emotions. I raised my eyes to Heaven and my lips murmured: "We ever thank you, our living and everlasting King." These words left my lips full of wonder and excitement. I also said the blessing: "Who has granted us life and sustenance and permitted us to reach this time," which is traditionally recited on joyous occasions.

"To wash! To sleep in a real bed!" we told each other with shining faces.

"Can you believe this dream has come true?" asked my sister.

And indeed, these simple daily needs are not accorded sufficient regard, as if they can be taken for granted, as if they are the inalienable right of every person....

*   *   *

My sister Lola was sent to the hospital. She weighed only sixty pounds and could barely walk. After Rivka visited her in Bad Werieshofen, she couldn't stop talking about the hospital: "Lola is lying in a clean bed!"

That same evening, Rivka ran a temperature, and she too

was "blessed" with confinement to a hospital and a clean bed.

Each day, my healthy sister Bela and I would visit our ailing sisters in the hospital. Transportation was irregular and unreliable, so we walked each day for several miles along a wonderful route where fruit trees grew on both sides of the road. All we had to do was stretch out our hands and enjoy the pickings.

We camped temporarily in the kitchen of the German who had saved us on the eve of liberation. Each night he would spread mattresses on the floor for us. The arrangement was to his benefit as well. Our staying there proved to the Americans that he was not a Nazi but that he had actually saved Jews.

Once we asked him if he knew of the existence of a concentration camp scarcely a mile from his home. He answered, "No, we knew nothing about it."

We lost no time in finding a room to which we could bring our sisters when they would be released from the hospital.

Seven survivors from Czenstochow, in Buchenwald after the liberation

Chapter Forty-five

The End of the War and the Search for Relatives

The war ended on May 7, 1945 — about six years after its outbreak on September 1, 1939. The German army was defeated on all fronts, while the civilian population lowered their heads and shut themselves inside their houses. It was their turn to be frightened, and for good reason. They understood full well what could be expected of a people persecuted and tortured as we had been, once their freedom is restored. However, they had no concept of the nobility of the Jewish soul. The blood of our loved ones, murdered and slaughtered at the merciless hands of the Nazis, called out for vengeance from the mass graves of Europe and from the smoke of the crematoria. However, we survivors were not capable of committing the kinds of acts that those human beasts had committed, though hatred and revenge burned in our hearts.

The day after the liberation of Turkheim, we returned to the camp and met with those who had remained. There, we set fire to the lice-ridden huts. Everyone able to stand on his feet danced around the flames. Then we sat for a long time around the bonfire and thought about the future. How should we organize ourselves? How could we search for our dear ones? Whom should we notify that we were still alive?

Daily life began, once more, to take on the rhythm of routine. The Occupational Authorities distributed refugee documents, which enabled us free travel by public transportation. Some people, beginning to recover from the trauma of their experiences, set up a kitchen in the one remaining hut at the camp. This was run by volunteers who were provided by the authorities with the necessary food supplies. We were given food coupons and came each day from the village to the camp for the midday meal. We walked the mile to the camp through green fields, with a song on our lips.

Each day, the stalks of wheat in the fields grew taller, and like them, my joy increased. A light breeze blew through the grain, bending it gracefully as if in prayer. Wild flowers, too, graced the fields and from afar they looked like a beautiful colored carpet. In the light of the shining sun, I felt that the world was beautiful once again, and now I, too, could enjoy it.

*   *   *

One day, a few of us girls went for a walk in the streets of Turkheim.

"What's that on the notice board?" I drew my friends' attention to a poster.

"Let's go and see."

On the notice board the Americans had hung photographs taken at the time of the liberation of the camps. One part of the poster showed what was discovered when the sealed cattle cars were opened: dead bodies, piled one on top of the other in a lifeless heap.

The second part showed the living dead, concentration camp inmates standing on thin legs in striped prisoners' garb. Headlines announced in German: "Germans, these are your crimes."

Three German girls came over to look at the pictures and giggled. "The Americans dug these pictures out of the ancient relics of Pompeii's earthquake," they said, smiling merrily.

We were appalled. Then, one of my friends, who had been searching the picture for her own relatives, went over to the Germans and slapped their faces as hard as she could.

"Perhaps now you'll start to believe!" she shouted.

*   *   *

When my sisters recovered somewhat, we began to travel in search of the missing members of our family, including the uncles, aunts, and many cousins from both sides of the family. But first and foremost, we wanted to find out what had happened to our sister Hela, whom we had left behind at Ravensbruck in February, our brother Pinchas Menachem, who had been sent to Treblinka in November 1942, and Chanoch, who had remained at Herby, a few miles from Czenstochow, on January 17, 1945, when they had separated the men from the women, sending us to Ravensbruck and him to another camp.

And perhaps, perhaps, we would find people who could tell us what had become of Father and our brother-in-law Shmuel. Perhaps, whispered a sneaking hope, they were alive and looking for us...?

For our darling mother, we did not look, nor for our little Yisroelik. We knew that they had been shot in the Czenstochow cemetery, and buried there in a mass grave.

At the same time, my brother-in-law Shmuel, who had also survived the war, was starting to look for us. He found a group of Jews at Landsberg, some fifteen miles from where we were living, and got help from them in tracing us. The survivors of the Turkheim camp had made a "list of the living" and circulated this to the other refugee camps which sprang up in various places, usually close to the sites of liberation.

Shmuel managed to locate us and one day appeared, with a bandage on his hand.

"The Americans bombed our camp and a splinter from one of the bombs hit my stomach. Fortunately, I was protected by the little pot for the daily soup ration, which I had tied around my body, but the splinter ricocheted, hitting my hand. One finger was badly wounded.

"Did you get medical help?"

"At the camp? Of course not!"

"And when you were liberated?"

"Yes, but that was several days later. Meanwhile, the finger had become infected and had to be amputated."

"What a shame!" we sighed.

"Even so," declared my brother-in-law, "the merits of our fathers stood me in good stead — the blood poisoning did not spread to other parts of my body. That, too, is something to be grateful for."

Now my sisters set off to visit every place where there was even the slightest chance of finding a family member alive. We carefully checked all the lists from the camps which were circulated to us. Unfortunately, these were not always accurate or updated. In Bergen-Belsen alone, 20,000 people had died since the end of the war! Many of them died from the sudden abundance of food, which they were unable to digest after such prolonged starvation. On the list of fatalities we found the name of our uncle, A. Schoenfeld.

We also found, on the list of survivors from Bergen-Belsen, the name of our brother Chanoch! My sister and I were now entrusted with the task of finding him and bringing him back to our family.

We set off. Buoyantly we promised our sisters and brother-in-law who remained behind, "We won't come back without him!" I added, "Don't worry about us, but be prepared for an absence of two to three weeks. Transportation is erratic, and we have very little money, which doesn't leave us with many options."

First, we traveled towards Munich. We knew that there was a large settlement of Jews there at Feldafing. We stayed overnight and asked the camp directorate, which included Rabbi Avrom-tche Ziemba, a cousin of our uncle, to help us in our search with whatever resources were available to them. In those days, the communication between Jewish communities was good, and members of the camps' directorates traveled around the country regularly, to help in the general search for relatives.

The next day a large car was to leave for Frankfurt, where there was also a large concentration of Jews, and we joined it.

At that time, Germany was divided into four zones: American, British, Russian, and French. Bergen-Belsen was in the British zone, and we therefore had to get special permission to enter. The directorate provided us with money for our journey, and at Frankfurt-am-Main, we boarded a train for Hanover, a large city about twenty miles from Bergen-Belsen.

We reached Bergen-Belsen about a day later. Here we were told, to our surprise, that a respected family from Lodz, the Cederbaums, which now consisted of a father and two sons, had "adopted" Chanoch, along with several other youths, making up a family which now included some twenty people! Mr. Cederbaum had received a nice house in the city of Stendhal, and they had settled there. To our great joy, he had left his forwarding address with the Bergen-Belsen directorate in case relatives came looking for any of the youngsters.

Worn out by our travels, we decided to stay overnight. "That way we'll gather new strength, and tomorrow we'll continue our journey."

The next day, we rose early and began another long trip, this time towards Stendhal, in the Russian zone.

We reached the town very late at night, and with beating hearts went to find the address we had been given. We found the house, but there was no response to our knock.

"No choice but to ask the neighbors," we decided, and went up to their door. They answered our question in the affirmative: "Yes, they used to live here."

"Where are they now?"

"Oh, they left a few days ago, traveling by night."

"Why? Did something happen?"

"When the Russians took over the town they were afraid that their house, property, and, most importantly, their stock of food would be confiscated. Someone told them about such a plan."

"So they left?"

"Yes. The head of the family took the food supply and fled!"

"Do you know where they went?"

"Yes. To Braunschweig — that's a large town in the British zone."

We left the house and looked at each other. "We had better hurry up and get out of here, too," we said with bated breath. We still had a few marks left, so we boarded a train. It began to move with that unique rhythm. Did another "surprise" of this kind await us at Braunschweig? If so, we would be stuck there without a cent to our names.

*   *   *

I will never forget that meeting with Chanoch. It was August, 1945, the height of summer. The weather was warm and pleasant. From the open windows came the strains of classical music and the sounds of friendly argument and laughter. We marched boldly up the long street, checking the numbers of the houses.

"Here's No. 85." My sister grasped my arm.

Another minute and we stood in front of a tall stone building, three storys high. Would we find here the family we were seeking? Would our brother, for whom we had yearned so deeply and had searched for so long, be here?

Our fatigue was forgotten, and my heart began to pound hard and fast as if it would burst with joy. I was full of happiness and excitement — and a certain amount of trepidation: would I recognize my skinny little brother of eight months ago? After all, he was at that age when boys change so fast. But there was no need to worry, my little brother Chanoch stood before us, so familiar, so beloved....

He, too, was very excited. He had been looking for us for four months. Only two weeks earlier, Mr. Cederbaum had received the Turkheim list, and Chanoch had been overjoyed to see that we, his "real" sisters (he had "sisters" in the new family, too) were included among the living.

We stayed overnight, and the next morning Chanoch parted rather sadly from his new family, to whom he had grown attached, and from Mr. Cederbaum, who had been like a father to him. We thanked him from the bottom of our hearts for having saved our brother and taken him under his wing immediately after the war had ended, when the camp was so polluted and full of illnesses. Mr. Cederbaum was the brother of a cousin of ours through marriage, and when he saw the name Chanoch Dziubas on the survivors' list, he realized that this was his sister's relative.

All the way back to Turkheim, Chanoch told us about his experiences at Buchenwald, where he had been sent in January 1945 when the Germans had separated us. He, too, had undergone many hardships and much suffering. He was fortunate that the Germans had stopped the transports to Auschwitz by that time, so that whoever was able to survive was saved, with the help of our Father in Heaven. Out of three brothers, only Chanoch survived to bear the family name.

On the list of camp survivors which came from Sweden, we found the name of our sister Hela. We were informed that after the liberation, women whose state of health was poor were sent to Sweden from Ravensbruck, Bergen-Belsen, and hospitals in Germany. Our joy was great. Thank God, Hela was alive, and for the moment it did not matter what state of health she was in. With God's help she would get proper care in the hospital, and she would soon get well and return to be united with us.

Immediately, we dispatched a letter to Sweden asking Hela

to write at least a few words as soon as possible and let us know how she was feeling. We asked her not to delay her answer a moment longer than necessary — we were waiting for her and, with God's help, would see her soon.

About a month later, a letter arrived from Sweden, from Hela Dziubas. We all gathered around, and my sister Rivka care-

The survivors from Czenstochow come back to the ruins of the ghetto.

fully opened the letter, shaking with excitement. The magic words passed from mouth to mouth: a letter from Hela!

Alas, to our sorrow, the letter was not from our beloved sister but from another woman who just happened to have the same name and birthdate. Mrs. Hela Dziubas wrote that she deeply regretted having to disappoint us, but the names of her parents were different and she did not have any brothers and sisters.

The smiles of joy froze on our lips. How sad that in a matter of seconds it is possible to swing from the heights of joy to the depths of such terrible grief.

We also searched ceaselessly for my father, traveling to every possible place where he might be found. We could discover no traces of him, nor of any of the people who had been with him.

Deep in my heart, Father remained alive for a long time afterwards. I simply could not resign myself to so great a loss.

His gentle and noble guidance followed me still in my new life. Always, I would hear an inner voice reminding me: "Father would not talk like that," or "Father would not have used that word," or "Father would not have acted in such an unseemly fashion"....

Epilogue

For us, the Holocaust was a nightmare of pain, fear, and suffering. We lost our beloved parents, two brothers and a sister, uncles, aunts, their children, and grandchildren. The process of accepting this loss was slow and painful, but throughout my life, even in the hardest moments, I never doubted for a moment the reality of God's rule in the world. Who can know and understand His ways?

Our world had collapsed as completely as if there had been a mighty earthquake; we were like Noah after the Flood. Nevertheless, I was relatively well off in comparison to others: I still had three sisters and a brother. Many girls whom I met were left all alone, abandoned, like a lone cactus in the middle of the desert, with no brothers, no sisters, no living kin.

Now that the Flood was over, we had to leave the Ark and begin a new life.

*　　　*　　　*

We remained in Germany, as Jews, for three years.

In the little town of Landsberg, about twelve miles from Turkheim, emerged a small kernel of an Orthodox Jewish community, consisting of three men. These were Chassidim of Gur who, like us, wished to return to their roots. After being forbidden to do so for six years, they once again grew their traditional beards and sidelocks and began to adhere to a strict standard of kashrut. Very soon, they were joined by other Jews, who shared their desire to reclaim their Jewish heritage, laws, and customs. It was no easy task. There were no books of Halachah (Jewish law) and no ritual slaughterers. Nevertheless, to our good fortune, a young man was found who was an expert in the art of ritual slaughter, and he was, to his great joy and satisfaction, soon burdened with plenty of work.

Just before the Jewish New Year, my sister and I were sent, chickens in hand, to Landsberg. The journey took two days with erratic transportation, and we walked long stretches of the route. When we got back home to Turkheim we brought an unheard-of attraction — kosher meat in honor of the first festival after the liberation!

In November 1945, after the High Holy Days, we moved to the town of Zeilsheim, close to Frankfurt-am-Main. Frankfurt, the great and famous city, had in the past been the home of a splendid and flourishing Orthodox community, which boasted such leaders as Rabbi Shimshon Rafael Hirsh, Rabbi Jakob Rosenheim, and Rabbi Breuer.

Now, we soaked up Judaism in the small Beit Yaakov girls' school opened by Mrs. Rivka Horowitz and Mrs. Rivka Engelard (pupils of Sarah Schenirer, the founder of the "Beit Yaakov" movement). Their lessons were interesting and instructive. I was also able to take intensive courses to receive a Matriculation Certificate.

When the State of Israel was established on May 15, 1948, my sister Bela and I emigrated to Israel. Here, too, I studied in the Beit Yaakov Teachers' Seminary, in Jerusalem.

Perhaps someday I will write about my life in Israel, how I established myself, with God's help, without financial assistance from anyone or from any other source, as I did not want to be dependent upon my fellowmen. Like the dove after the flood, I preferred the bitterness of the olive leaf given by God to the luxuries

The Torah center in Frankfurt-am-Main that the Nazis destroyed

provided by flesh and blood. Perhaps I will also write about my marriage and about our family, which is the continuation of my father's home in Czenstochow.

It is my hope that my story will deepen my readers' understanding of life, and will help them to recognize the good in life and to appreciate everything as a gift of grace from God.

And if one of my readers learns to see his glass half-full rather than half-empty, and to trust in the Creator of the world, that will be my reward.

Appendix I

Chronicles of Czenstochow

There are indications that there were Jews in the city of Czenstochow as early as 1794, in the days of Stanislaw August Poniatowsky, King of Poland (1764–1794).

In the year 1806, the army of the principality of Warsaw — established by Napoleon on the ruins of Prussian Poland — managed to conquer the Fort of Czenstochow. From reports of the period we know that at that time almost 4000 people lived there, of which 500 (or 12.5 percent) were Jews.

It is also known that at the time of Prussian rule there was a Jewish community in Czenstochow. Documents were found from the period which tell of Jewish life, community organization, and work.

In the year 1830 many Jews emigrated to Czenstochow, which was conveniently located. There are strong indications of Jewish participation in local industries.

When "special areas" were designated for Jewish residence in Poland, Czenstochow followed suit. Only a very few of the richest Jews lived in non-Jewish areas. In 1862 the "special areas" were abolished, and the Czenstochow City Council was very proud that it had taken this step *de facto* two years before the official abolition. From then on, Jews were free to settle in all parts of the city.

The first synoagogue was built in Czenstochow in 1787. The Jewish population increased, and forty-five years later an additional synagogue was built with a study house (*beis midrash*). A great deal of money was collected for this purpose, and the construction was very rapid. This synagogue stood for over one hundred years, until its destruction by the Nazis in 1939.

A modern synagogue was built in 1900. I remember that on November 11, 1938, on Poland's Independence Day, our school went there to hear a sermon about freedom. This synagogue was very grand, its great hall lit by crystal chandeliers and its walls and ceiling decorated with beautiful paintings.

At the time of the first revolution in Russia, in 1905, the Poles got permission from the Russians to hold elections. In Czenstochow, there were the same number of Jewish as non-Jewish candidates. Already there were anti-Semites who tried to prevent Jews being included in the list of nominees for election.

A fine community life then flourished in Czenstochow. Apart from the many synagogues of all kinds, there were handsome public buildings which served the needs of the Jewish population: a hospital, orphanage, old age home, and academic and trade schools. The hospital was staffed entirely by Jews, and it had very high standards and the best available medical equipment. The hospital was known for its excellent and dedicated treatment of patients.

There was also a special "Hospitality House" where Jewish travelers could eat and spend the night. In the same building there was a study house where the poor could study and pray and were given other help of all sorts.

Czenstochow was a city of Torah scholars in the fullest sense. It had rabbis, Jewish judges, ritual slaughterers, and outstanding scholars. In the evenings, young men and old would gather together in one of the many "*stiebelach*" (rooms set aside for prayer) and enthusiastically study a page of Gemara. From

1919, a Jewish newspaper, *Der Yid*, was printed in the city.

Cultural life was lively and plentiful, and the community prospered. Young people from all over the region looking for work and Torah found them in Czenstochow. Among the many yeshivos (schools of higher Jewish learning) the largest was Siftei Tzadik, named after the Rebbe of Pilitz. This great scholar had lived in Czenstochow for many years, and after he passed away his students established the yeshivah in his name.

The population of Czenstochow included people of all political persuasions and classes. There were many professionals: doctors, lawyers, and engineers. They often studied in universities at Warsaw or Krakow and then returned to Czenstochow. They all had work and, since the town developed rapidly, were in great demand. The Jews contributed significantly to this enormous development.

Jewish social and public activity was particularly lively and varied. There were many clubs — associations which represented the different streams of opinion where high-level political discussions were conducted. The Warsaw press of the period testifies to this. Of the provincial cities the two most frequently mentioned are Lodz and Czenstochow.

My birthplace, then, was attractive both inwardly and outwardly. The local Jews were kindly folk, concerned for their fellowmen and willing to sacrifice everything for their neighbors. Communal life was pleasant and fulfilling, with much productive activity. The pulse of our town beat day and night in all aspects of communal life: religion, culture, and mutual aid in all its forms.

May the memory of Czenstochowians, martyrs of the Holocaust, be forever blessed.

Appendix II

Scandinavia

Since I have already mentioned Sweden, it seems to me appropriate to write about that country and its neighbor, Denmark, which was occupied by the Germans during the Second World War.

The miracle of the rescue of the Jews of Denmark was already legendary in its own day (it took place in October 1943) and was a small ray of light and hope, shining in the moral gloom and darkness that had engulfed Europe. The rescue of Danish Jewry aroused the admiration and praise of the free world for the brave nation which had fallen under Nazi occupation.

Jews settled in Denmark from the seventeenth century onwards. The Danish government of that time was interested in Jewish settlement from Portugal, since Portugese Jews were renowned for their wealth and international commercial connections. However, very few Portugese Jews actually reached Denmark, although at this time other Jews, from Ashkenaz-Germany, began to settle there.

In the nineteenth century, the Danish Jews received emancipation and enjoyed full and equal civil rights. By the second half of the nineteenth century, Jews were very much involved in Danish society. This was a time of national crisis due to Denmark's defeat in the wars against Prussia and Austria, and the Jews played an important part in the rebuilding of the Danish economy. They opened banks and became an integral part of the economic and social life of their country. This integration, or assimilation, resulted in a striking number of mixed marriages, which reduced the number of Jews by some 50 percent.

During the years 1901–21, waves of refugees from Eastern Europe reached Denmark, almost all of them victims of the pogroms which took place after World War I. The Chief Rabbi of Copenhagen came to the aid of the refugees and asked the Danish authorities for permission to let them settle there, a request which was generously granted. Most of the Jews settled in or around the capital, Copenhagen, while a few moved to smaller centers.

In March 1939, while Germany declared a ban on her Jewish residents, prayers were being said in the great synagogue at Copenhagen to celebrate the 100th anniversary of its founding. King Christian X personally participated in these prayers, his noble presence and impressive bearing arousing great joy and admiration in the hearts of all those present.

Denmark was not spared the fate that also befell many other European nations and, together with Norway, was invaded by the German navy on April 9, 1940. The invasion took the Danes by surprise, since less than a year earlier, in May 1939, the Germans had signed a non-aggression pact with Denmark. The cunning Nazis justified the invasion as part of their wish to "protect" Scandinavia from an anticipated Anglo-French attack.

"You must agree to accept the protection of the Third Reich," announced the German governor to the Danish foreign minister. "As long as you accept our protection, the Reich will not — now or in the future — injure the territorial integrity of Denmark, nor interfere with the political and economic independence of the Kingdom."

"But we are neutral," protested the foreign minister.

"Of course, of course," the ambassador placated him with a smile, "Go on being neutral."

* * *

The democratic Danish regime continued without a break for three and a half years, until August 29, 1943. Although to all outward appearances the Germans maintained the status quo, negotiations were carried out throughout the period between Denmark and Germany, which required unilateral compromises on the part of the Danes. In spite of this, the government and the nation as a whole managed to maintain the integrity of their country, its productive economy, and the determined spirit of the people. The Danes put their whole being into maintaining the constitution which ensured the freedom of the individual, fraternity, and equal rights for all citizens, regardless of race, religion, or ethnic origin.

The Germans permitted the Danes to go their own way, since they had their own reasons for wanting to keep the peace. Meanwhile, they thoroughly established themselves in Denmark and exploited the economy and its products for their own purposes. However, they could not forgo their racial theories for long. They had already tried to pass anti-Jewish legislation in 1942 but then accepted the advice of the German governor that outright persecution of the Jews in Denmark would mean the failure of the policy of negotiated compromise.

In 1942 the governor demanded that Jews should be removed from key positions. Simultaneously, an order was issued to arrest individual Jews on the grounds that they had committed political or civil crimes. The protector was a cautious man and did not want to take drastic steps since he understood that a policy of "little-by-little" would be more readily received be the Danes. Eventually, they would become accustomed to the fact that some citizens were being deprived of their rights. Draconian measures could only lead to resistance — after all, the ruling elite, led by the King himself, as well as the common people, were totally opposed to anti-Semitism. At the time, the Germans were interested in postponing the inclusion of Danish Jewry in their

"Final Solution" (i.e., to the "Jewish problem"), which was then getting under way.

In August 1943, this "humane" attitude ended and the Danes were confronted with an "iron hand" policy. Even when it went against his own best interests, Hitler could not endure for long any tolerant policy towards the Jews: "There has been enough appeasement of the Jews," he shrieked at a meeting of his High Command in Berlin. "Get rid of them!" The verdict was deportation, and it was to be carried out on the 1st and 2nd of October, 1943.

The German occupation command in Denmark wanted to avoid the deportation, at least for the time being. They protested to their superiors in Germany that there would be a popular uprising and that Danish public opinion would never allow it to happen.

"What will happen is that we will lose their cooperation," warned the German ambassador, "and there is no doubt that the supply of basic food stuffs from Denmark to Germany will be hurt."

*   *   *

Amidst all this, news of the forthcoming deportations filtered through from individual Germans who had Danish friends. These in turn hastened to transmit the bad news to the Jews. Many Danes tried to acquire entrance permits for their Jewish friends to neutral Sweden, which was willing to take in refugees. Then, at the end of August, 1943, exit permits for Jews wishing to leave Denmark were stopped altogether.

Now, only one possibility remained: a secret escape. This was not easy, because the much-vaunted German efficiency proved itself once again in Denmark. German patrols roamed the streets and kept an eye on what went on. Fear and terror reigned in Copenhagen when on August 29, 1943, the Germans arrested the leaders of the Jewish community. In order to minimize the impression that the measures were aimed solely at the Jews, a number of Danish gentiles, known to oppose the Nazis, were also arrested. No sooner had the iron cooled, however, when the next day, August 30, a search was conducted in the offices of the Jewish community, and the register of Danish Jews was confiscated. This sounded a warning note for the Jews. When the mechanism of German deportation went into action, the blood froze: everyone knew what that meant.

Previously, only a few Jews had realized what was happening and went into hiding. Others simply could not admit what was going on around them. For these Jews, the deportations came like thunder on a clear day and caused them unspeakable anguish. They had known what was happening elsewhere in Europe. They had heard about Jews being forced to wear the yellow star, about expropriation of property, and the intolerable conditions in the ghettos. They had also learned about the planned "final solution" for the Jews of Europe — and beyond. They did not believe that the honest, decent Danes, who acted only in accordance with principles of law and justice, would turn them in to the Germans.

Until August 1943, most of the Danish Jews were relatively well-off. They were not parted from their property, nor turned out of their apartments, but continued to live normal lives. For most of the time they had difficulty in realizing the magnitude of the threat that now hung over their heads. Even so, the leadership of the Danish trades unions did not rest: "You don't understand the situation," they warned the Jewish community leaders. "This time it's really serious, the pressure from Berlin has gotten worse, and the Germans really mean to carry out the policy they set in Eastern Europe. Don't waste a moment!"

The Jews were finally convinced of the seriousness of the situation. The rumor spread among all the Jewish families, and they began to leave their homes and to hide with Danish friends. The Danes opened their homes, and even strangers spontaneously did their best to save Jews.

The Jewish leadership did not have faith in the ability of the Danish authorities to protect the community, and this seriously damaged their own ability to improve the situation. The community was in disarray, since the leadership could not bring itself to act in such a way as to be able to rescue the Jewish population.

At the time, the director of the Danish foreign office was a Mr. Svenigson. He immediately approached the German protector in Denmark to ask that the deportation of the Jews be postponed.

"The Jews are enemies of the Reich," replied the protector, "and as such, we must send them to camps in Germany."

"In that case, we could keep our Jews in camps here in Denmark," suggested the director.

"Yes, I'll check out the idea. I'll cable my superiors," came the answer.

Only later was it discovered that a cable was indeed sent, but instead of a request to hold the Jews in Danish camps, it included information regarding the first "consignment" of Jews, which left by sea on October 1, and included 202 people. Another overland transport (by train) included eighty-two men and one woman.

*   *   *

On October 2, 1943, the radio broadcast a short, dry announcement which said: "Action has been taken against the Jews and they have been removed from the population."

This laconic statement shook the Danes out of their tranquility. The whole nation was shocked, and it was decided to take action with the help of the Resistance. The criminal act of the Germans stirred the depths of the Danish soul, arousing rage and resistance. The time had come for action.

German patrols with the confiscated register of Jews in hand, made a systematic house-to-house search. Where there was no answer, they burst locks and broke down doors. Sometimes they would go and search at the house of a neighbor to find out if they knew anything of their vanished Jewish neighbors.

The Germans' thin veneer of good manners soon cracked and they behaved with characteristic crudeness. They entered a Jewish old-age home and began to drag the elderly residents out by force, hitting and kicking them with smiles on their faces. Some were taken to the synagogue where they were "interrogated" regarding the whereabouts of Jewish "saboteurs." The others were taken straight to a German ship anchored in the harbor.

The Danish population was stunned. In one night everyone was up in arms. The terrible, cruel truth now revealed to them was intolerable. The Danes simply could not accept the idea that the Jews, an integral part of the Danish people, could be treated in this way. The new situation encouraged the Danes to unusually daring and brave activity. The trades unions and the Resistance came up with a daring rescue plan. The whole nation united with one supreme goal: to come to the aid of the innocent Jews.

In the first stage, schools and hospitals were placed at the disposal of the refugees, and the best doctors offered their help. Bisperg, the largest hospital in Copenhagen, turned itself overnight into a huge center for stowaways. The organizers of the rescue were afraid that the secrecy of the operation would be damaged because of the large numbers of people involved, and that they might somehow be discovered by the Germans. Thus, they found all kinds of pretexts to "hospitalize" the refugees and organized several "funerals" in order to justify the large number of people present in the hospitals, without arousing German suspicions. When the rescue team was informed that the Germans were on their tracks, the nurses suggested that since their residence was close to the hospital, the stowaways should hide there.

The entire staff of this huge hospital was involved in the rescue of the Jews. The daring plan was to smuggle them over to Sweden — a plan fraught with danger and difficulty.

On October 1, the Germans had published orders forbidding the use of small boats, which had to be stored in a given location. Presumably the Germans wanted to close the last possibility of escape before the deportation.

Almost the entire nation was feverishly engaged in organizing the mass escape. The actual plan was entrusted to the fishermen, some of whom still had boats available. The refugees were hidden in private homes along the coast and waited for the signal that the ferries were ready to depart. They were terrifed that they would be caught by the Germans.

Fishermen, police, and border police all cooperated in the operation. Information was passed from one to another by means of codes and passwords. According to these signs, the fishermen knew when they could safely set out for the open sea, the most favorable route, and at which point they could land.

The passengers were deeply frightened. Some of them were hidden in the storage hatches, others among fishing equipment. The shores were patrolled by the Germans, and rescuers as well as rescued were in danger of their lives. At night, the Germans would illuminate the sea with searchlights and terror would seize the escapees and the fishermen.

But step by step, boat by boat, with deep courage, improvisation, and daring, the Jews were transferred to Sweden. The organizers exploited every possible opportunity for rescue. Cargo vessels that sailed loaded with wares for Germany hid dozens of refugees among their goods. Each captain sailed off his usual course and approached the Swedish coast in order to transfer escapees to a waiting Swedish ship. These rendezvous usually took place on the high seas and were planned in advance. The Swedes would come towards the Danish ships, receive the Jews, and transfer them to Sweden, "the safe shore."

As soon as the ship — ferry or fishing boat — reached the Swedish territorial waters with its live "cargo," both rescuers and rescued could breathe freely again.

Their marvelous rescue operation succeeded thanks to its organizers, who were mostly from the Danish intelligentsia. Yet the whole nation was spontaneously involved and everyone played their part. The Danish people acted speedily, firmly, and with exceptional daring and courage. All the rescuers believed in the justice of their humanitarian deed. Even the police did not wait for instructions but followed the dictates of their own conscience. After the deportations of the Jews, they realized that the Germans were amoral law breakers and did everything they could to help the Jewish refugees, who were innocent of any crime.

*   *   *

The story of Denmark and Sweden proves conclusively that it was not easy for the Germans to carry out the "Final Solution" without cooperation, or against the will, of the people amongst whom the Jews had settled. Without the active cooperation of the police, and the people, in the lands under Nazi occupation, the picture might have looked very different. Admittedly, the objective conditions in Denmark and Sweden were different from those prevailing in, say, Poland or the Ukraine. There was the proximity of a neutral state willing to receive the Jews, and a relatively small Jewish population — only 2 percent of the Danish population as a whole.

The Danish and Swedish people will be recalled in Jewish history as righteous gentiles and as a shining example of courage to all mankind.

The Clear Light of Faith

Penina Margalit
columnist, author, and educator
(reprinted from HaModia)

What is that light in Ruth Zeidman's very special book? The "darkness" is the darkness of the Holocaust, a thick darkness which came down upon the world and took away all brightness and light.

But what is the light to which the name of this book alludes? Ruth Zeidman's autobiography is a story of pain and suffering, of parents losing children, and children losing parents. Darkness!

And, in spite of everything — even in the darkness — a light does shine, the clear light of faith, with which the author made her painful way. Even in the valley of tears she sensed the light of Divine Providence on all sides. We hear the echo of prayer and thankfulness all along the weary way. This light shines and sends its spiritual rays through the darkness which threatens to stretch from horizon to horizon.

Herein lies the uniqueness of the book *A Star in the Darkness*. On the one hand, we have a picture of the harsh reality of the

Holocaust through the horrified eyes of a young girl, who was suddenly taken from her warm and happy home; yet on the other hand, we see a rich spiritual heritage, which cannot be overcome by the darkness of the new reality. The instinctive nobility of the daughter of a well-bred family did not disappear even under sub-human conditions of suffering, humiliation, hunger, and shame.

In a confused world, where bestiality reigned unchecked, the light of the refined Jewish spirit shines. Sublime values of family solidarity, devotion to one's fellows, the renunciation of the "I", shine in the valley of the shadow of that awful tyranny, of the embodiment of evil, of rampant wickedness and deeply - rooted hatred.

A little light, sending rays of spiritual brightness into the gloomy swamp of darkness. The natural delicacy was not crushed under the rough jackboots; the warmth and feeling were not destroyed by the terrible frost of stony hearts.

The book "A Star in the Darkness" has a powerful educational message. It proves that the conditions of life do not dictate human behavior, and that man's spiritual possessions cannot be choked, even when the spiritual air seems to have run out. From the storehouses of the past, from the resources of hope for the future, an oxygen of values may be drawn. Even with the faltering legs, the starving body, and the awful weightlessness of the *musselman*, tremendous bravery can be demonstrated by guarding a personality formed by good hands, in a struggle against immoral norms, by flying the flag of humanity above the ruins of the collapse of cultural and human values.

Although this book unsparingly presents us with a terrible reality, there is, despite it all, a certain thread of poetry which runs through it. This is a book which tells the hardest story of all but which contains, alongside all this, a poem to a newly opened flower, to skies of blue peeping through a fragment of cloud, to friendship that overcomes cruelty and alienation.

The book contains a sweeping optimism which stands in contradiction to the outer reality, but which is in harmony with the refined inner self. It has the great light of eternal faith, that many bitter waters will not wash away. And that is the message of this book. Like all works on the Holocaust, it requires us to "recall what Amalek has done to you," it tells of atrocities, but always presents the noble and unconquerable Jewish spirit as a foil to these horrors.

6 August, 1984

Zachor Association

Honored Lady!

First of all, congratulations on your important contribution to the documentary literature of the Holocaust. To our regret, and to our great shame, many of our fellow Jews wish — and try — to forget and to obliterate the heritage of the Holocaust. And if I say "heritage," I mean that same wonderful greatness of spirit and dedication of soul that Jews revealed in that awful time as, for instance, the last piece of bread that your noble father gave to the beggar at his door.

It is to be regretted that until today the general tendency of historians has been to research the Holocaust focusing on Germany, among the vilest of all nations, and not on the greatness of spirit manifested by the Jews. The Zachor Association tries to remedy this distortion, with the few resources at its disposal.

With admiration and blessings,

Yehoshua Eibeschitz
Chairman
"Zachor" Association for Commemoration of the Holocaust

How, Against All Odds?

A review by Atara Samuel
Ministry of Education and Culture
Dept. of Pedagogy
Curriculum Division
History Teachers' Newsletter, #2
Jerusalem, 1990

Thirty-seven years after its seemingly final closure, Ruth Zeidman opens the reel of images engraved in her memory during the Second World War.

In her book, *A Star in the Darkness,* she depicts forty-five of those images. Her vivid descriptions take the reader on a voyage back in time, as she experiences, through the eyes of young Rutka Dziubas, all that transpired in her life from the time that the Nazis took over her hometown, Czenstochow, until the conclusion of the war.

On the surface, *A Star in the Darkness,* is a memorial to the author's family; to the community of Czenstochow; to those who suffered and perished in the concentration camps; to all of European Jewry during the bleak period. But *A Star in the Darkness* is designed to touch the reader on a much deeper level. The reader becomes involved, not only in the events which took place, but also in young Rutka's battle to preserve her values and integrity, as she struggled for her very existence.

Ruth Zeidman provided clear, concrete answers to the repeated questions of wondering readers: "But how, against all odds? From where did she get the strength? What *was* her 'star in the darkness'?"

In the introduction to her book, she openly declares the purpose to which she first opened the "reels of memory," chose from it those images which she chose, and put them into writing. In her words, "May it teach the reader...to believe in a better future, to strengthen our souls, and to trust in the Creator of all."

This lesson is deftly woven throughout each and every one of the forty-five chapters of this book. It is felt in the many acts of mutual assistance and perseverance described, in the expression of heartfelt emotions and desires as prayers of gratitude and supplication, and in the conclusions she reaches as a result of her experiences, both at the time that they occurred and years later, while writing the book. For example: "In any situation, a person can always be happy...if he only looks downward, at all those whose situation is worse than his. For sorrow and joy have no boundaries, and are subject to no absolute laws"; or "Even when I fainted, I did not give in, and never ceased to fight."

"*A Star in the Darkness*" is appropriate as a background text for a course of study on the Holocaust in a junior high school history class.

The similarity in age between the students and young Rutka will certainly strengthen the students' interest in the subject.

If the book is read as part of an integrated course of study, moral dilemmas can be brought for classroom discussion, through the stories of the merchandise of the First World War, the poor man in the doorway, Mrs. Goldman's necklace, and others.

The Ministry of Education recommends that this book be included on the teaching syllabus in every school in the State of Israel.

HOLOCAUST MEMORIAL CENTER

Ruth Zeidman's memoirs "Light in the Darkness" is a chilling, and yet uplifting story of a young girls experiences and reactions to the events of the Holocaust during the Holocaust. I strongly recommend this book for schools and the general public interested not only in the events of the Holocaust, but also on the reactions of a young girl to her own plight and that of her family and people. The compassion and humanity of Ruth Zeidman in an environment when inhumanity and barbarism was the norm is most uplifting, and is bound to have a salutary impact particularly on the young readers during their formative years.

Rabbi Charles H. Rosenzveig

Founder & Executive Vice-President

6602 W. Maple Road, West Bloomfield, MI 48322-3005 (248) 661-0840 Fax: (248) 661-4204
Internet Address: http://holocaustcenter.org